"In *Rooting for Rivals*, Peter and Chris have captured God's heart for true Kingdom-minded ministry! They've created an irrefutable case for leaders around the globe to work together for the greater good. The truths in this book have the power to literally change the world!"

—Mark Miller, vice president of high performance leadership, Chick-fil-A, Inc.

"Peter and Chris have captured the heart of donors in *Rooting for Rivals*. We want the ministries we support to work well with others to maximize the impact of scarce resources for the Kingdom. Every nonprofit leader should read this book and follow its call to action."

—Greg Brenneman, executive chairman, CCMP Capital; Emmy Award-winning author of *Right Away and All at Once*; and former chairman, Burger King and Continental Airlines

"I really thought, when I first saw the title of this new book, that I was already pretty good at treating my rivals in a godly manner. But these fellows never let us off so easily. Set your plow a little deeper, and get ready to think in some fresh ways."

—Joel Belz, founder, *World Magazine*

"*Rooting for Rivals* is full of practical and compelling guidance for effective partnership in and out of the church—a reminder that the scriptural counsel to look not only to our own interests but also to the interests of others applies even when those interests are closely aligned."

—John Inazu, author of *Confident Pluralism*

"This book is a must-read for any who would dare to sacrifice personal ambition for the sake of the Kingdom. In a society where narcissism is the new normal, Greer and Horst call us back to the mind of Christ, to leadership in humility."

—Daniel Rice, author, and founder, #Gospel

"While people would naturally think rivalry is confined to non-profits, there is often just as much among foundations and donors. Everyone wants to back a winner, and sometimes we unintentionally encourage ministries not only to compete but to become rivals. We are part of the problem. We need this book!"

—Fred Smith, president, The Gathering

Books by Chris Horst and Peter Greer

Mission Drift (with Anna Haggard)
Entrepreneurship for Human Flourishing
Rooting for Rivals (with Jill Heisey)

Books by Peter Greer

The Board and the CEO (coauthored by David Weekley)
The Giver and the Gift (coauthored by David Weekley)
Created to Flourish (coauthored by Phil Smith)
40/40 Vision (coauthored by Greg Lafferty)
The Spiritual Danger of Doing Good (with Anna Haggard)
Watching Seeds Grow (coauthored by Keith Greer)
Mommy's Heart Went Pop! (coauthored by Christina Kyllonen)

ROOTING
» FOR «
RIVALS

HOW **COLLABORATION** AND **GENEROSITY** INCREASE THE IMPACT OF LEADERS, CHARITIES, AND CHURCHES

PETER GREER AND **CHRIS HORST**
WITH JILL HEISEY

BETHANYHOUSE
a division of Baker Publishing Group
Minneapolis, Minnesota

Published by Bethany House Publishers
11400 Hampshire Avenue South
Bloomington, Minnesota 55438
www.bethanyhouse.com

Bethany House Publishers is a division of
Baker Publishing Group, Grand Rapids, Michigan

Paperback edition published 2019

Printed in the United States of America

ISBN 978-0-7642-3125-4 (cloth)
ISBN 978-0-7642-3165-0 (trade paper)

Library of Congress Control Number: 2017963594

Cover design by LOOK Design Studio

Authors are represented by Wolgemuth and Associates.

19 20 21 22 23 24 25   7 6 5 4 3 2 1

Dedicated to the leaders who believe
in a world of abundance,
not scarcity.

And to our HOPE International colleagues,
clients, partners, and donors.
We are privileged to serve alongside you.
Thank you for loving and serving
in the way of Jesus.

You're blessed when you can show people how to cooperate instead of compete or fight. That's when you discover who you really are, and your place in God's family.

Jesus, THE MESSAGE[1]

Contents

Foreword

I t's not about you."

I wish I had embraced this piece of wisdom sooner as a young campus minister with InterVarsity Christian Fellowship. I was not well-known among my colleagues for being a team player. I liked being a pioneer, a lone ranger, a one-man show. I liked figuring things out on my own and being a trailblazer for a new generation of nonwhite missionaries. It worked for me, and my name quickly rose in national prominence.

Fresh out of college, I didn't want to serve an existing Inter-Varsity chapter, so I planted a new one on the Harvard campus. And because the results exceeded expectations, I quickly solo-planted another chapter at Boston University, and eventually in three other states. I wrote papers, manuals, and a book that detailed how to effectively do campus ministry, *without* consulting any peers. One of the biggest discipleship moments of my early marriage came when my wife, Nancy, and I were asked to co-direct a summer program in Vietnam. "Co-direct? What's that?"

Intentionally working alongside others was not my top priority. I sincerely wanted to serve the Lord. I urgently wanted to rescue lives being lost and to transform campuses needing renewal. I earnestly wanted more students to follow Jesus into world missions. But, deep down, something else was true—maybe even more true: *my ministry was all about me.* My work. My gifts. My reputation. My success. I needed to learn that this wasn't the way God intended for His Kingdom to operate. So God sent me to an unreached country halfway around the world for four years, so I would see how He was using *other workers* to accomplish His purposes. To discover how much I *needed them.* To wonder if I was as much their "mission field" as the people in that country.

As I began repenting of my selfishness, pride, and independence, I began learning to embrace the upside-down Kingdom values that Jesus proclaimed—humility, generosity, and interdependency. As I began dying to my own name, I began living to see only *Jesus'* name being lifted high.

The idol of "me and mine" is deeply ingrained in all of us and our individual organizations. Its fingers are wrapped tightly around the generous, joyful life God wants us to live, and it squeezes a little tighter each time it feels threatened. Let others work with you to accomplish God's mission? *You'll look weak or unnecessary if you let others help.* Cheer for those you're competing with? *You'll never get your time in the spotlight.* Help someone become more successful than you? *You and your ministry will be supplanted. Is that what you want?*

Those questions will always persist. But after twenty years in campus ministry, and with each step into a new leadership role, I've shed more and more of my lone-ranger tendencies and embraced the importance of generous collaboration. I've learned a key lesson for any leader in faith-based work: Building the Kingdom of God is a team sport, not a competition. We're better together, not apart.

It would be easy for my fellow campus ministry leaders to look at one another as competitors. After all, we are doing similar ministry, driven by similar goals, and sometimes working at the same campuses. We might assume that there are only so many students to go around and perhaps, if we were being honest, so few donors to go around. We could easily adopt an "us vs. them" mentality. According to the values of the world, we should be competitors. We should view one another with wary skepticism, as threats to our individual success and possible disruptors of what we individually want to do. Yet the values of the world don't dictate how we view one another; the values of God's Kingdom do. We aren't competitors in a limited marketplace. We're partners in God's mission! When this truth captivates our hearts, it pushes out any sinful tendencies toward selfishness, pride, and independence.

Twice per year, Nancy and I join the presidents of five other campus ministries, along with their spouses, for a weekend of fellowship. I treasure these times. We carry each other's burdens, pray, and cheer each other's successes. We invest in each other by sharing what we're learning in our own leadership challenges. We have become friends and partners. In recent years, our commitment to partnership has also led to growing friendship and partnership among our key leaders. Vice presidents of operations, leadership development, fundraising, field ministries, and marketing meet annually in their respective groups to share best practices, new ideas, and common struggles. On the surface, it seems like a risky idea: Why would we share our most intimate struggles or our most successful strategies? Can you imagine two professional sports teams taking a joint retreat in the middle of the season? Or the CEOs of Microsoft and Apple taking a break from their battles for marketplace dominance to encourage one another and swap ideas?

We do this to model our commitment to the apostle Paul's words in 1 Corinthians 3:7, 9 (NIV): "Neither the one who plants nor the one who waters is anything, but only God, who makes things grow. . . . For we are co-workers in God's service." We do this because we're on the same team. We're servants of God's mission. When one of us succeeds, we all win, because Jesus' name is lifted up on campus.

It's not about me. Embracing this truth has prepared me to lead InterVarsity toward a new season of generosity and partnerships. As I write this, there are over one thousand college campuses with no discernible student ministry. Millions of students lack the opportunity to hear the gospel or to join a Christian community on campus. In the past, we might have waved a halfhearted "Good luck!" to our peer organizations while trying to reach them by ourselves. No longer. It's not about planting organizational flags or making organizations great but about advancing God's mission and declaring God's name to be great on these unreached campuses. We're working together to mobilize intercessors. We're designing platforms to give away our best ministry insights and tools to anyone who wants to minister on campus. We're sharing technology and working together on legal challenges. We're asking one another: "What would happen if we stopped caring who was bigger, or better, or the most well-known? What could we accomplish if we stopped competing and started partnering? What needs to happen so that every corner of every campus hears the gospel?"

When Peter and Chris invited me to write this foreword, I marveled at God's sense of humor. It wasn't that long ago that I wasn't even aware of other workers, much less rooting for them. Today, I find myself in roles that are primarily about advocating for and helping others advance their missions. As president of InterVarsity and as a trustee of Fuller Seminary,

I steward ministries that develop and prepare the next generation of leaders for other organizations and the Church. As a trustee of a Christian foundation, I channel financial resources to other ministries. As a senior leader, I invest much of my time mentoring younger men and women to accomplish *their* calling. I urge you to study this book and take it to heart. *Rooting for Rivals* is a call to a fresh vision for our organizations and churches. It's a road map to embedding a spirit of humility and generosity in our hearts and in those of the teams we lead. And it's a field guide to the sins that bedevil our best attempts to partner and mire our ministries in lone-ranger thinking. You will find parts of it challenging or convicting. I certainly have. But I suspect you'll also find, like I have, a renewed passion for God's people to work together as one body in Christ.

You're in good hands. God has used Peter and Chris's book *Mission Drift* to equip thousands of faith-based organizations, including InterVarsity, for better Kingdom service by keeping them Mission True—radically focused on Christ and His mission and deeply committed to keeping the gospel as the center of their work.

For as long as I've known them, I've benefited from the deep wells of wisdom and humility that God has dug in their hearts. I'm grateful for their long history of leadership and for their willingness to share the lessons they've learned, even ones that have come the hard way. And I'm inspired to see how God's Kingdom will advance as more organizations and leaders take the lessons of this book to heart.

It's not about you or me. Thanks be to God!

—Tom Lin, President and CEO,
InterVarsity Christian Fellowship

Introduction

Amid the process of writing *Mission Drift* several years ago, I (Peter) was returning home from a conference in Cape Town, South Africa, when I saw Wess Stafford—someone I deeply respect—across the airport concourse. At the time, Wess was the president of Compassion International, one of the largest nonprofits in the world. In terms of organizational size and reputation, he was Michael Jordan, and I was the kid shooting hoops at the park waiting for his growth spurt. Wess was a keynote speaker at the conference, where he not only presented but also was bombarded during meals and in the hallways by people eager to have a few minutes with him.

He must have been exhausted.

As he sat at the airport, reading a book and presumably beginning to relax, I awkwardly approached him, like a fan seeking an autograph. After a bumbling introduction about how I appreciated his leadership, I asked if I could ask him a few questions. His response exuded uncommon generosity, "Of course! Would you like to sit down?"

He had no idea who I was, yet he gave me his undivided attention. Putting his book away, Wess answered my questions and showed genuine interest in our conversation until it was time to board the plane. He responded with patience and thoughtfulness. It was clear that he was doing more than just trying to help; he seemed eager to know me and to cheer me on in my own journey. He embraced the mission I described as though it were his own, and his entire posture seemed to offer, "How can I serve you?"

Although we had just met, he was rooting for me.

When we began discussing the causes of mission drift, he shared freely from his experiences. Displaying unusual openhandedness, he offered to share any of Compassion's documents and manuals that might be helpful in our research. There was absolutely no expectation of reciprocation and certainly no benefit to him from sharing.

Though HOPE International is far smaller than Compassion, we are also a faith-based international nonprofit. Many donors give to both HOPE and Compassion. In many respects, we could be considered rivals.

> **RIVAL:** a peer organization appearing to compete for funding, staff, or recognition.

Even though we worked at different organizations, Wess graciously offered assistance. In retrospect, it wasn't just Wess who modeled this type of radical generosity. This attitude prevailed among the exemplary leaders we interviewed in *Mission Drift*.

They consistently went out of their way to help. Though they were busy leaders, they always seemed to make time. They shared openly about their models and missions. They answered our questions, and our follow-up questions, and our follow-up-to-the-follow-up questions. They seemed to have nothing to hide from us, no proprietary information or trade secrets. They gave with no strings attached, and talked with us without any expectations we would feature them in the book. They actively pursued our good and not just their own.

It was as if they had a calling and passion that superseded their organization—that helping *us* was in some way part of *their* mission. They acted as if we weren't leaders of rival organizations competing for funding or recognition but friends on the same team working toward the same goal. They cared deeply about the work they do, but at the core, these leaders seemed to think more about the Kingdom and less about their organizations.

These encounters with Wess and other Mission True leaders left a lasting impression. We were inspired by these leaders who are more animated by advancing God's Kingdom than merely building great organizations.

This point, which we almost missed, is significant. Beneath the very best Mission True organizations are leaders who believe they have a calling beyond building their organizations. They see themselves as part of a much bigger team pursuing a much bigger mission.

They root for their rivals.

Work Appears and Then Vanishes

Just 28 percent of the roughly fifty thousand nonprofits that obtained tax-exempt status in the United States in 2005 reported financial activity a decade later.[1] In just ten years, roughly three out of four nonprofits ceased to exist. A mere eighty-five organizations have endured five hundred years or more.[2] The remaining millions of organizations closed, merged, or experienced some other demise. They are gone.

This list of shuttered institutions includes all types of charitable organizations—schools, hospitals, shelters, youth ministries. Odds of survival are slim.

This morbid reality is important for all leaders to acknowledge. Our work is "a mist that appears for a little time and then vanishes."[3]

Even the most talented leaders and brilliant business plans will have faded from memory fifty years from now. We've authored this book for men and women working in Christian faith-based nonprofit organizations of all varieties, though we hope others will benefit from it as well. For these leaders, the prospect of being forgotten should not lead to discouragement. Christians understand the mist we are. Our organizations, endeavors, strategies, initiatives, and plans will one day fade from relevance.

We will be forgotten.

This might seem like an odd case to make in a leadership book. If our organizations will one day vanish, why care about leading more effectively? If it's true most of our organizations will be forgotten, won't that drive us to focus exclusively on maximizing our own prosperity or trying to secure some sort of enduring legacy? If it's true our organizations will not last generations into the future, why do the hard work of building infrastructures, raising funds, creating strategic plans, and innovating? Why deal with difficult employees or disgruntled donors?

For Christians, the answer is clear. We are not just building organizations. Our success is not defined by where we stand in relation to our "rivals" or how long our name endures. We are participating in an eternal Kingdom. We are members of a community not marked by organizational boundaries but by the blood of our Savior.

As a result, we have a different, cruciform view of *winning*. Up-and-to-the-right growth is not the only metric for success for followers of the One whose legacy on earth was defined by self-sacrifice and love for those who could never repay Him. In that light, rooting for rivals—cheering on and coming to the aid of those the world sees as our competitors—doesn't feel all that crazy. Hundreds of years from now, our descendants will likely not know our names, nor those of our organizations. But if we successfully embrace the unity Jesus taught, our descendants will remember what the Church did together.[4] They will remember that this generation continued the work of bringing good news to the poor, proclaiming freedom for prisoners, and setting the oppressed free.[5] They will remember that the gospel was translated into every language, racial injustice was confronted, and extreme poverty was eradicated.

If our descendants talk about us, they will talk about the miraculous ways God worked in and through the Church to bring hope, truth, compassion, and joy to our world. We can imagine no greater success.

Organizations come and go, but we are part of a movement that has no end.

Mission Not Drifting: Now What?

This book is for leaders who are untroubled about whether their names or organizations will be remembered five hundred years from now, whose ambition extends beyond themselves. For those who can join A.W. Tozer in his prayer, "Make me ambitious to please Thee even if as a result I must sink into obscurity and my name be forgotten as a dream."[6] For leaders who anchor their work to the things that endure forever and elevate their vision to something bigger and better than building an organization.

This is a book for leaders obsessed with making the name of our God great and entirely unconcerned about making their own names great—and for those who aspire to become that type of leader.

Mission Drift exposed a troubling reality within faith-based organizations: many are at risk of losing their purpose and the very thing that makes them unique. As we encountered the risks of drift within our organization and conducted our research with hundreds of faith-based organizations of all varieties, we heard the same story again and again. Faith-based organizations were forgetting why they existed. The irony was that for many *faith*-based organizations, faith was slowly becoming irrelevant.

We've realized since writing *Mission Drift* that even if we get our own proverbial house in order, our broader mission will fail miserably if we stop there. We've come to believe that no matter how many guardrails we put in place or how many bylaws we draft to fend off drift, faith-based organizations cannot be Mission True unless they exist for a purpose beyond their organizational borders.

Seek First

Jesus reminds us in clear language to "*seek first* the kingdom of God and his righteousness, and all these things will be added to you."[7]

To do this as leaders of faith-based organizations is much harder than it might seem. Because of how deeply entrenched we are in cultural values of winning, competition, and owner-ship, we regularly lose sight of how radical our organizations would be if we were truly to *seek first* the Kingdom of God.

And this, in short, is exactly what we mean by challenging readers of this book to *root for* their *rivals*. Because in the curious, upside-down way of the Kingdom of God, God converts our competing into rooting and our rivals into allies. *Rooting for Rivals* is an invitation to reject territorialism in pursuit of a higher, more compelling mission. To fundamentally alter the posture and practices with which we love and serve, based upon our shared core commitments as followers of Christ. To view our organizations not as grand murals but as pieces of a mosaic created by and for our Master Artist.

Rooting for Rivals is an invitation for faith-based organizations to be known for outrageous generosity and openhandedness, as we collectively pursue a calling higher than any one organization's agenda. It's an invitation to live not as warring clans but as people of a united Kingdom. To reject comparison and rivalry and pursue collaboration and friendship.

The goal of this book is to equip leaders of faith-based organizations to become exceptionally generous leaders through a posture of radical openhandedness. The first three chapters share *why* we should root for our rivals. The remainder of the book focuses on *how* we root for our rivals, as we wage war on the sins that cause us to become isolated and insular actors starring in our own small plays. The path forward, we'll argue, demands we name the "sin which clings so closely"[8] and pursue a life of personal and organizational virtue.

We can write this book only because we are beneficiaries of leaders who have modeled this posture in our lives. We could fill a chapter with names of leaders who have shown radical concern with *our* success, regardless of whether they stood to benefit from it personally. These leaders—forebears and peers at fellow faith-based institutions, donors, professors, and pastors—have inspired this book, and many of their stories inhabit it.

Better Together

Looming high above busy Broadway Avenue in downtown Denver stands a historic mansion that until recently was rapidly losing the grandeur of its youth. Years of neglect had resulted in the once-pristine brick Victorian's slow conversion into a neighborhood eyesore and a hotbed of drugs, violence, and other illicit activities.[9]

But when Derek Kuykendall stumbled across the property, all he saw was potential. As executive director of Providence Network, a faith-based transitional housing organization, he believes in redemption stories. Through a series of remarkable events, Providence Network purchased the home with plans to rehabilitate it for men and women rebuilding their lives.

But they did not go at it alone. Kuykendall desired to do more than expand the boundaries of his organization.

"Our friends Matt and Nikki Wallace lead Dry Bones, an organization serving Denver's homeless street youth community," Kuykendall shared. "Together, we began to dream about what it might look like if we brought multiple organizations together under one roof."[10]

Providence Network didn't specialize in youth homelessness. Dry Bones didn't specialize in transitional housing. But they're now learning from each other as they serve one of Denver's most vulnerable populations in the restored mansion.

In this flophouse-turned-home, twelve formerly homeless youth now live in community with six staff members—a team drawn from both organizations. To further support their residents, Providence Network and Dry Bones have partnered with Purple Door, a nonprofit coffee shop and roastery focused on employing and training at-risk youth. Together, these three faith-based organizations leverage each other's respective strengths and fulfill their mission more effectively than they ever could apart. This joint venture is a picture of institutional humility, each organization recognizing its own strengths and limitations and celebrating the power of partnership.

"At the Dry Bones fundraising banquet, Matt Wallace invited me to share about Providence Network. He welcomed me up, lauding all the great things about my organization," Kuykendall said. "Anyone that works for a nonprofit knows how crazy that is. He invited me, the executive director of a 'competing' organization, to share about *our* work at *their* gala. That just isn't normal. It doesn't happen."[11]

When the mansion was still under renovation, I (Chris) took a tour. With each step, I grew increasingly excited. Kuykendall was right. What was happening under this roof was entirely abnormal. It was remarkable. But I began to wonder what might be possible if this spirit of collaboration *became* normal. What might happen to our communities—and to us—if this sort of partnership wasn't surprising?

It's our hope that *Rooting for Rivals* will help propel this sort of partnership into the realm of normalcy. In this book, we hope to provide a window into the virtues and practices of openhanded and extraordinarily generous leaders—and examine how these virtues can percolate into and reach beyond our organizations. We hope to demonstrate why rooting for rivals brings life to you and your organization and fosters enduring impact for the Kingdom. We also hope to provide practical examples and case studies to guide you in living out these principles and bypassing potential landmines.

We hope you'll join us in rooting for our rivals.

» PART ONE «

WHY WE ROOT FOR RIVALS

CHAPTER 1

Our Uncommon Unity

For faith-based organizations, the landscape is rapidly changing. The Pew Trusts assesses confidence Americans place in our fifteen largest public institutions. The military and small business rank highest. Congress and big business rank lowest.[1] When they began doing the survey in 1973, 43 percent of Americans said they placed a "great deal" of trust in "the church or organized religion." Today, just 20 percent do. In 1973, just 7 percent said they placed "very little" trust in the church. Today, 24 percent do. Over the past few decades, the percentage of Americans who trust the church has been cut in half. And the number of those who strongly distrust the church has more than tripled.

Governmental pressure has also increased. Over the last decade, Pew Trusts states that the United States has moved from a country of "low" religious freedom restrictions to "moderate" restrictions.[2] Faith-based mentoring organizations, homeless shelters, universities, and international relief and development organizations feel this surge in suspicion.

Some of the increasing mistrust results from changes in our culture, but some is a direct indication of our own state. The

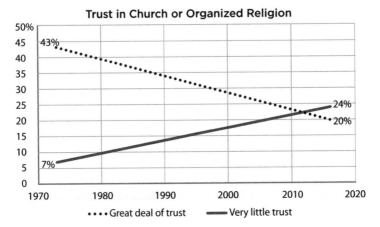

Trust in Church or Organized Religion

•••• Great deal of trust   ▬▬ Very little trust

world has seen celebrity pastors, faith-based nonprofit leaders, and priests abuse their power, fall into moral failure, and purvey their influence for unseemly political aims—breeding well-deserved suspicion and skepticism. As Beth Moore wrote, "The enemy's hope for Christians is that we will either be so ineffective we have no testimony, or we'll ruin the one we have."[3]

Trust in faith-based organizations is also eroding for a subtler but equally dangerous reason: When our organizations embody a rugged individualism and fuel division between people intended to be united in mission, we deserve the world's skepticism. When we act like we're entirely disparate organizations—each responsible for ourselves alone—it confuses the culture around us. When we concern ourselves only with our own organization's success, the world wonders, *Are you on the same team or not? Are you allies or rivals? Why such division?*

United We Stand?

In our culture, division runs rampant. We disagree—often passionately—on politics, church, sexuality, science, and so many other issues.

We feel the tension in our homes when we gather at the Thanksgiving table or around the tree at Christmas. We hear the division in daily shouting matches on the news. We scroll past it—or engage in it—on social media. Every year, we are becoming more and more divided, with several research studies concluding our country has not been this polarized and divided since the Civil War.[4]

And within Christian faith-based organizations, we feel it acutely. Intuitively, we know we're supposed to be on the same team, but reality tells another story. If we are at all unified, it's probably in our agreement that we are a nation and a Church divided. Fragmented, really.

Guidestar lists nearly eighty-five thousand nonprofit organizations in the United States that self-identify as Christian.[5] "The Center for the Study of Global Christianity counts forty-five thousand denominations around the world," wrote Jennifer Powell McNutt in *Christianity Today*, "with an average of 2.4 new ones forming every day. The center has an admittedly broad definition of *denomination*, but even a dramatically lower count will be absurdly high in light of Jesus's prayer in John 17 that we all might be one."[6] In 1 Corinthians, Paul chastises Christ's followers in Corinth who have split into four groups: "Is Christ divided?"[7] What would he think of forty-five thousand?

John 17—Jesus' longest recorded prayer in Scripture—rebukes the present situation of the Church. Its main theme is the unity of Jesus' followers. He prays "that [we] may become perfectly one," so that the world may know the Father's love.[8] The implication is that our witness to the world hinges on our unity.

"Christ's prayer for unity and endurance is formed, uttered, and accomplished at the greatest hour of trial in all of redemptive history," writes K. A. Ellis. "At this critical juncture there is one relationship on his mind, and it is ours."[9]

Jesus says our oneness is the way that others will identify us as His followers: "By this all people will know that you are my disciples, if you have love for one another."[10] Yet as clearly as Jesus prioritized unity among His followers, we are quick to disregard it. Our natural inclination is to splinter. For Protestants, *protest* is in our very name. In our tribe, when disagreements emerge, we split.

There are important and legitimate reasons for churches to split and organizations to define strong boundaries. There is a time to separate. But there is an opportunity for Christians to find unity even in disagreement. There is an opportunity for us to build bridges across the lines that divide us. In this bright age of individualism, intellectual property rights, and splintering denominations, our unity in Christ is fading.[11] But, "How good and pleasant it is when brothers dwell in unity!"[12]

The unity of God's people is the first reason we can and should root for our rivals. And when we consider the power and beauty of what we hold in common, sometimes our divisions seem almost trivial.

What Color Is Your Buggy?

I (Peter) live in Lancaster County, Pennsylvania, where tourism—a booming local industry—is driven by a fascination with the Amish. Visitors arrive to observe this community, intentionally set apart from technology and modern dress. Tourists dine in Amish homes, take buggy rides, and tour working farms. In some ways it's like visiting Colonial Williamsburg and seeing a snapshot of life frozen in time, but these are not actors. Very real convictions motivate their eschewal of modernity.

The modern-day Amish have their roots in sixteenth-century Europe, where their ancestors faced extreme religious persecution. They were so strong in their convictions that thousands were martyred, being burned at the stake, drowned, and beheaded. The Amish arrived in North America in the eighteenth and nineteenth centuries. Shaped by their experience of persecution as well as their understanding of Scripture, they established a life and culture set apart from the larger society. Soon it wasn't enough to be separate from the outside world. Even within the Amish community, schisms formed. Once they were no longer persecuted, they seemed to turn against each other. What most Lancaster County tourists don't realize when coming to see "the Amish" is that they are encountering many distinct groups.

At the beginning of the twentieth century, there were three or four affiliations. By 2012, there were more than forty, not including smaller subgroups. Rifts among the groups have been caused less by issues foundational to the faith than by matters such as the use of buttons and zippers. Churches have split based upon a disagreement between those who wear two suspenders versus one suspender, and then split again over whether the suspender should fall across the right or left shoulder.[13] The division can even be spotted in the buggies. While driving through Amish communities, you may come across black, brown, yellow, and white buggies. Each color is an external sign stating, "We are not like *them*." It signifies a separate Amish or Mennonite church faction. The Byler Amish are distinguished by their yellow-roofed buggy, the Nebraska or Old School Amish for their white-topped buggy, and the Peachy Amish for their all-black buggies.[14]

"You have to get the most powerful magnifying glass to see the hairs that resulted in the splits," reflected Charlie Kreider, a friend who grew up in the Mennonite Church in Lancaster County.[15] Disagreements over the letter of the law run through the paint, proving that just about anything can drive a wedge between families and friends of the same faith conviction.

Our propensity to divide runs counter to Jesus' prayer for unity and propels us to root against our rivals. And these somewhat arbitrary distinctions can have deadly consequences.

Calipers, Nursery Rhymes, and Emblems

Several times over the past few years, I (Chris) have visited the Kigali Genocide Memorial in Rwanda. The first exhibit in the memorial displays an ominous image. At first glance, the picture is innocuous enough. It is far less grisly than many of the pictures throughout the rest of the memorial. But it is far more haunting.

In the picture, a Rwandan man sits in an examination room. A Belgian examiner measures the width and length of the man's nose with a metal caliper. He then measures the eyes of the Rwandan man, contrasting and comparing the shape and size of the man's eyes to a chart of various cultural eye shapes.

We now know that following World War I Belgian colonizers sent scientists to Rwanda, wielding "scales and measuring tapes and calipers, and they went about weighing Rwandans, measuring Rwandan cranial capacities, and conducting comparative analyses of the relative protuberance of Rwandan noses."[16]

These tools, though far less violent than the machetes and guns used to perpetrate the genocide, are far more barbaric. They were used to draw distinctions and grant favored status to Rwanda's Tutsi minority, who were seen as more evolved (i.e., more European), while the majority Hutus became oppressed and increasingly resentful. When walking through the genocide memorial, jarring images of soldiers and militants line the walls. But it is this seemingly benign activity—a scientist wielding a caliper—that created division and preceded the slaughter of nearly one in ten Rwandan people.

First the calipers and scales were dispensed. Soon the common physical appearances of the Hutus and Tutsis were codified. Then, beginning in 1933, government officials mandated Rwandans record these differentiations between Hutus and Tutsis on identification cards. As the genocide unfolded, perpetrators used these cards and physical differentiations to separate neighbors from each other. To separate friends and groups of students from their peers. To determine who lived and who died.

At the memorial, the second floor exhibits the terrible realities of genocides committed across the world and across history. In each case, division precedes violence. The Nazis forced Jewish men, women, and children to adorn their clothing or an armband with the Star of David. Turkish military and government officials organized the genocide against hundreds of thousands of Armenians who were identified as Christians on their national identification cards.[17]

My family recently lived in the Dominican Republic for a few months. There, we learned about the history of Hispaniola and some of the horrific massacres carried out against ethnic groups on the island. In 1804, Haitian dictator Jean-Jacques Dessalines murdered all French residents who were unable to sing a Haitian nursery rhyme in Creole.

In a horrific turnabout, in 1937, Dominican dictator Rafael Trujillo commanded his troops to round up dark-skinned people living near the Haitian border. Once they did so, journalist Michele Wucker recounts that the soldiers held up sprigs of parsley and asked, "'What is this thing called?' The terrified victim's fate lay in the pronunciation of the answer."[18]

If the victims were unable to get the Spanish just right, they were killed and thrown into the Dajabón River, known commonly as the Massacre River in commemoration of the thousands of people who were killed because of their inability to say *perejil*—parsley—correctly.

Massacre River flows between the Dominican Republic and Haiti. This geographic divide is emblematic of the many divides we create between ourselves. Caliper or nursery rhyme. Badge or identification card. These create borders between us, separating men and women from each other, signifying those who have more (and less) worth.

As Christians, we unequivocally reject these symbols and signs of superiority, affirming that all people have been created equally in the very image of God. But, believers and unbelievers alike, we are quick to form divides and take sides.

Contrived Competition

Social psychologist Christena Cleveland shares about a 1954 social experiment titled "The Robber's Cave" by Muzafer Sherif.[19] The study explored what would happen if you take a group of homogenous and healthy kids and put them in a position of focused competition with each other. The 1950s were a period of such social experiments, and Sherif and his team gathered a group of eleven-year-old boys and told them that they were going to have a summer at camp. This became a summer-long experiment on creating conflict and managing hostility.

Gathering at a major state park in Oklahoma, the teams spent two weeks together bonding and forming their organizational identity. One group chose the name the Rattlers and the other group chose the name the Eagles. When the groups were brought together, Sherif posed as the camp handyman and observed what happened as they created a greater sense of competition among these boys.

Remember, this was a homogenous group of boys who were *randomly* assigned to different teams.

While the boys initially got along well, the competitions became more intense. Tug-of-war. Sports. Games where there would always be one winner and one loser. The winning team received prizes and recognition at meals. The losing team seethed. In a matter of days, the mood of the camp turned dangerously hostile. The Rattlers raided the Eagles' cabin. The Eagles torched the Rattlers' flag and began collecting rocks to throw at their opponents. The atmosphere grew so hostile that the boys had to be forcibly separated. How quickly these boys identified with their clan and were willing to do anything at all to the other! The teams were randomly assigned, yet they quickly became rivals willing to do whatever possible to tear the other down.

It might seem absurd to think of professionals, and particularly faith-based leaders, behaving the same way: Team Methodists vs. Team Lutherans. Team clean water vs. Team Bible translation. World Relief vs. World Vision. HOPE International vs. Opportunity International. Thankfully, we aren't in the habit of torching one another's property, but we wonder if our rivalry wiring is so deep that we often act like the Rattlers and the Eagles. If we're honest, we might be just as quick to throw stones—even when we'd objectively agree the other group is doing important, Kingdom-building work.

After hearing two nonprofits describe each other as rivals, Jeff Rutt, entrepreneur and philanthropist, reflected, "They are choosing the wrong enemy!"[20] When we think of other organizations as our competition, we are choosing the wrong villain. We *should* fight and struggle—but not against one another. The competition is poverty. The foe is injustice. The opponent is our own sinfulness. The enemy is the evil one. "For we do not wrestle against flesh and blood," Paul writes, "but against the rulers, against the authorities, against the cosmic powers over this present darkness, against the spiritual forces of evil in the heavenly places."[21]

We believe in the power of competition. In both the private and social sectors, organizations can propel their peers toward greater effectiveness and efficiency. But it's so easy to forget that these peer organizations are not our opponents. Competition against one another is just as contrived as the Rattlers battling the Eagles, and it distracts from our true battle.

What if we were to believe that there was another way of looking at the world? What if our faith compels us to discover such a different worldview?

As people united in Christ, we are invited to dramatically expand our definition of "us" and ensure that it extends across organizational, political, racial, and denominational divides.

"Very soon we will find it difficult to sustain the metaphor of the 'body of Christ,'" said Ajith Fernando, author and Youth for Christ Sri Lanka teaching director. "We believe in 'a lot of bodies' of Christ . . . [but] there is one body of Christ."[22]

What if we believed, like Fernando, that there simply are no competing teams within the body of Christ? There is either one body or there is not. Embracing this worldview would make our witness, our friendships, and our impact exceedingly greater.

For followers of Christ, "Winning is when we are united, not when one has won and the other has lost," Fernando argues.[23]

We believe the increase of external pressure on faith-based groups might provide an unexpected opportunity to rediscover our unity in Christ. As the culture around us in this country grows increasingly suspicious of and unfamiliar with our faith, it provides a new opportunity for Christians to share and show what we are *for*. To lead and serve differently. To focus on our unified mission and tenaciously pursue it. To do more together than we ever could do alone.

From Competition to Collaboration

In this new cultural moment, there are trends accelerating an opportunity for Christians to better work together. Perhaps the most salient among these trends is the belief among academics, grantmakers, and nonprofit thought leaders that solving the big problems in our world will depend on organizations working in collaboration with, not in isolation from, one another.

"No single organization is responsible for any major social problem, nor can any single organization cure it," wrote John Kania and Mark Kramer on the *collective impact* trend in the Stanford Social Innovation Review. "Large-scale social change requires broad cross-sector coordination."[24]

Mike Brock, chief strategy officer at Transforming the Bay with Christ (TBC), couldn't agree more. Convinced that churches and nonprofits could do more together than alone, Brock hoped to systematically address homelessness in the San Francisco Bay Area. TBC began gathering Bay-area Christian leaders across various domains—including technology, innovation, business, and churches—to collectively build models for holistic and systemic change.[25]

Brock shared, "We've gathered forty-six different organizations to collectively study the factors of homelessness and figure out how we can collectively address this growing epidemic."

Knowing that God is already at work in the area, TBC sought out people, churches, and organizations already serving. "We don't want to usurp the work that God is already doing in our cities," Brock said. "We want to add to it." One of the first ways they addressed homelessness was to actively pursue job creation, recognizing underemployment and unemployment as key contributors to homelessness.

Teaming up to pioneer new employment opportunities in the Bay Area, Brock first connected with former NASA engineer Paddy Brady. Brady had retired at a young age after working on the International Space Station and the Hubble Space Telescope. Since that time, he had founded a faith-based nonprofit that specializes in bringing solar-powered appliances to communities in Malawi in an effort to promote self-sufficiency. Brock challenged Brady to create a long-term, sustainable job solution for the homeless far closer to home.

"What about an LED solar factory in the Bay Area?" Brady asked.

Modeling a Kingdom-centered, collaborative approach to addressing homelessness, TBC joined forces with Brady and his friend Tom McClellan to found Bright Vision Solar, the first LED solar factory in the San Francisco Bay Area created exclusively to employ the homeless community. As a result, formerly homeless men and women know the dignity and security of earning a living wage.

For years, Brady helped out at soup kitchens to serve the homeless, and McClellan donated clothes to those most in need. But when they collectively tapped into their gifts, callings, and talents for the Kingdom of God, the results were much greater than they could have imagined, and surpassed what they could have done on their own.

To reach more people impacted by homelessness, TBC has also extended their partnerships to create aquaponic and hydroponic gardens to help grow nutritious food for the formerly homeless population. They've also gathered forty-one churches across the Bay Area to share God's love in word and deed with the men and women served through these programs.

As TBC works collaboratively with Christian leaders across various domains to effect lasting, holistic change, it is reaping the benefits of treating peers not as opponents but as friends and partners. Intentional collaboration allows us to participate in more significant initiatives with far greater impact.

The Power of Pretzels

To compete or partner aren't the only options. While our instinct may be to push "competitors" away, there is strength in choosing proximity. We have to look no further than Hollywood (entertainment), Silicon Valley and Austin (technology), and Napa Valley (wine) for examples of competitors thriving in and through proximity.

Lancaster, Pennsylvania, where HOPE International is headquartered, is also home to Sturgis Pretzels, the oldest commercial pretzel company in the country. In almost every small town in Lancaster (believe us: we're regular partakers!) you can find pretzel enterprises large and small baking away, even though the local market is saturated with competitors. Since its founding in 1861, the pretzel industry has exploded into a half-billion-dollar industry. Over 150 years later, 80 percent of pretzels sold in the United States are still made in Pennsylvania.[26]

Harvard Business School professor Michael Porter described the benefits of this type of proximity in his seminal essay on cluster theory in 1998,[27] but in our digital age, this proximity is possible even when organizations aren't based in the same city. Popular among the creative industries, specifically, are the slogans "rising tide society" and "community over competition." These trends are popular hashtags, but they are more than that. They capture an ideal among emerging entrepreneurs.

And, they've resulted in the launch of Rising Tide Society, a network of photographers, web designers, visual artists, and other artisanal entrepreneurs all rallied together under this banner.

The entrepreneurs endorsing this movement openly share their business plans and their Rolodexes, and cheer each other on. Today, the Rising Tide Society comprises four hundred chapters across the world with tens of thousands of members.[28]

"We're all in this together . . . big dreamers, risk takers, and ground shakers," wrote Natalie Franke, a wedding photographer and founder of Rising Tide Society. "Leadership doesn't have to be lonely. It doesn't have to mean going at it alone."[29]

In the technology and software development world, the trend toward *open-source* development—in which developers make their source code freely available for others to study, alter, or distribute—has moved from a nascent idea to an industry mainstay in just decades.[30]

These trends define the new way leaders see the world. Collective impact, open-source, cluster theory, and *community over competition* are all ideas coined outside of the Church. If leading organizational thinkers believe this is true without sharing a bedrock of faith, how much truer should it be for those of us who do?

The Invitation

As followers of Jesus, we are all invited to join God's story of restoration. Jesus taught His disciples to pray for God's Kingdom to come and His will to be done not only in heaven, where all is new, but here on earth, where the consequences of the Fall are ubiquitous. The Son of God secured our redemption, but restoration is an ongoing work. As Christ's followers, we have the opportunity to work as one body to reclaim *shalom*: peace, flourishing, the world as God created it to be. That is a grand mission and it necessitates our unity.

We've entered a time when the Church is no longer associated with love and compassion but rather judgment, condemnation, and infighting.[31] We're no longer known for the sacrifice or humility Jesus modeled but rather for hypocritically failing to look beyond ourselves and our issues. If we want this to change, it's time to focus on our unified mission above our organizational agendas.

We need to look beyond our nonprofit boundaries to catch a glimpse of a bigger and bolder vision of the Kingdom of God. Our organizations are small players in a much more significant story. Understanding this story and the imperative of unity among followers of Christ should help us to do more than just get along.

Partnership won't always be the answer. Partnerships are difficult and can even be unwise. Just because two faith-based organizations work in Zambia doesn't always mean they should work together. Partnership can be a philosophical, geographical, or strategic impossibility. But even when we decide against partnership in a formal sense, it's always possible to assist one another by sharing resources, knowledge, or connections. It's worth investing the time to thoroughly consider opportunities that could help us step more fully into our shared calling of furthering God's Kingdom.

When we consider coming alongside others, we can go beyond just *fighting* extreme poverty to thinking about *ending* extreme poverty. Beyond rescuing young girls and boys from human trafficking to putting traffickers out of business. Beyond translating parts of the Bible into just a few more languages to translating the entire Bible into every language.

It's time to reaffirm a higher allegiance than the logo adorning our business cards. We are not just people working for organizations. We are not on rival teams. In Christ, we are brothers and sisters united for all eternity.

We're not claiming this is easy, and the stories to come are filled with our own struggles and shortcomings as well as the successes we've discovered from other organizations. We can tell you from experience that there will be disagreements and differences of opinion as we work together. In the words of author Scott Sauls, "Sometimes it takes having differences, not understanding one another, and even being a little bit irritated by and bored with one another, to remind us that the Church is a family and not a club."[32] But just as healthy families help one another grow, in the best, most life-giving partnerships "iron sharpens iron."[33] Those involved accomplish far more together than the sum of their independent efforts.

We are a family. We are one body. And we root for our rivals because the unity we hold in Christ is thicker than blood. But this is possible only if we understand the magnitude and upside-down nature of the Kingdom of God.

REFLECTION QUESTIONS

1. What does the world see when looking at the Church and parachurch organizations?
2. How are our actions toward others helping or hindering our collective impact and witness?
3. Who do you see as your competition and why? What would it take to view this "rival" as an ally?
4. What "rival" might benefit from closer collaboration?

CHAPTER 2

Kingdom over Clan

As he was building the McDonald's empire, Ray Kroc famously commented, "If any of my competitors were drowning, I'd stick a hose in their mouth and turn on the water,"[1] and "This is rat eat rat, dog eat dog. . . . You're talking about the American way of survival of the fittest."[2]

For some, there's nothing more American than a McDonald's burger and the belief that this is a dog-eat-dog world. We are to obliterate our competition.

Kroc's views on competition underscore the leadership philosophy many have embraced. But recent trends like open-source software and cluster theory highlight the merits of collaboration over competition. This alternative perspective guided winemaker Robert Mondavi, natural foods proponent John Mackey, and vacation rental entrepreneurs Dave and Lynn Clouse, cementing their stature as icons in their respective fields.

The Birth of Napa Valley Wine

"Your competitor is your ally."[3]

The opening words to Robert Mondavi's sales manual underscore the uncommon philosophy of the leader who "forged a revolution not only in Napa but also across the country, transforming the way Americans buy and drink wine."[4]

Born in 1914 to Italian immigrants to the United States, Mondavi had winemaking in his genes. His father and brother were also winemakers.[5] After working with his brother and father for two decades, Robert struck out on his own in 1966, when he founded Napa's first major winery since Prohibition.[6] Committed to excellence, he built his winery after visiting the most famous wineries in Europe and talking to the global experts in the industry.

Mondavi could have hidden his discoveries from his compatriots in California, attempting to grow his winery alone. After all, wouldn't it be better for business if his wine were superior to the other vineyards' around him? Isn't this survival of the fittest? But Mondavi did something unheard of: he invited owners of the surrounding rival vineyards to his vineyard and shared with them what he had just learned.

Mondavi's generosity extended beyond his fellow vineyard owners. Over the decades he lived and worked in the winery business, he led many "mission tours" throughout the region to create awareness about the burgeoning wine movement in Napa.

After Mondavi's death in 2008, his son Tim said his father built strong personal ties with many winemakers. "He developed friendships with other [winemakers] and exchanged ideas with many people. Not only did he learn from them but we shared what we had learned."[7]

Why would he share with his direct competition all the valuable information he'd just spent years gathering? He could have used his new-found expertise in wine-making to outperform every winery in the country. Why didn't he?

Mondavi believed in a bigger vision than owning a great winery. He wanted the entire Napa Valley to be known as an exceptional wine region. His vision expanded beyond the boundaries of his vineyard.

In *Entrepreneur* magazine, Tracy Byrnes writes that Mondavi "pushed Napa Valley to up its standards and compete with the world. He supported everyone and shared everything he had."[8]

His vision was not merely about his own vineyard.

Mondavi's generous, openhanded leadership approach succeeded beyond what he could have hoped. Today, Napa Valley is *the* American wine destination. Amateurs and sommeliers from around the world descend on Napa to experience the movement Mondavi started by helping his competitors win. The mission of Napa Valley hasn't been achieved by one singularly successful winery. The collective work and collaboration of the valley's winemakers, propelled by Mondavi in the 1960s, made it possible. Robert Mondavi saw beyond his winery's boundaries.

As Mondavi learned, unity is no easy task. There will be times when we succeed, building something beautiful and offering the world a glimpse of something grand, even ethereal. There are other times when our efforts are undone by pride, greed, vengeance, and other destructive behaviors that swiftly destroy what we have labored to build. This was the case for Robert Mondavi, whose family fractures caused the board to assume control of the business and sell the company in 2004 when he was ninety-one years old.[9]

Though he wasn't without flaws, Mondavi is considered the Father of Napa Valley because he thought beyond the property border of his vineyard, working toward a more expansive mission.

The Birth of the Healthy Food Movement

John Mackey was a self-described hippie. Living in Austin, Texas, in the 1970s, Mackey looked the part. He sported a shaggy, curly mop of a hairdo and adorned his face with a horseshoe mustache. After dropping out of college, Mackey decided he wanted to take on corporate America, specifically targeting the tycoons controlling the food industry.[10]

To do so, he launched a nonprofit health food co-op called SaferWay (a not-so-subtle jab at Kroger's Safeway grocery chain). But over time, Mackey grew convinced his tiny co-op could not make a dent in how Americans eat. So, like Mondavi, Mackey began to think beyond the walls of his co-op. To change the industry, he'd need to launch a full-on grocery store.

In 1980, Mackey decided to approach his top rivals to gauge their interest in collaborating. He met with Craig Weller and Mark Skiles, owners of SaferWay's competitor, Clarksville Natural Grocers.[11]

"I pitched them, 'Look, we're going to open this first natural foods supermarket, one of the first natural foods supermarkets anywhere in the world, why don't you do it with us?'"

Like Mondavi, Mackey saw his competitors as his potential allies. Unlike Mondavi, though, Mackey saw an opportunity for them not only to operate autonomously together but also to cofound a bigger and better endeavor entirely.

So they did. They merged their stores under one roof and chose a new name—Whole Foods Market. The natural foods movement was born.[12] Over the next thirty-seven years, Whole Foods Market expanded to 460 stores across the United States, Canada, and the United Kingdom.[13]

In 2017, Amazon bought Whole Foods for $13.7 billion, marking the beginning of a new chapter.[14] In just a few decades, the healthy food movement graduated from tiny cooperatives catering primarily to young, hippie enclaves in Austin to the most innovative force in the food industry in the West. John Mackey's healthy food vision is today officially mainstream, thanks to his belief in collaboration rather than competition.[15]

The Birth of the Vacation Rental Industry

Dave and Lynn Clouse did not aim to create a global phenomenon. They just aimed to help their neighbors.

In the early 1990s, Dave, Lynn, and their neighbors faced a dilemma. The Clouses owned a modest vacation home in Breckenridge, Colorado, but they grew weary of advertising in expensive vacation magazines and paying a local property manager up to half of their rental revenues. Still, they had few other options to reach vacationers. So each year they advertised in a skiing magazine with a small, three-line classified post with no pictures.

With the advent of the Internet age, Dave and Lynn saw an opportunity. They started small by creating a simple web page advertising their home with a few lines of text. Then they offered to do the same for their Breckenridge neighbors—for free. As Internet technology improved, Dave and Lynn started adding more homes in more places. Soon they figured out how to add pictures to their site.

One by one, the Clouses published vacation rental listings from all over the country, including competing vacation options to their own, on their website. Eventually Dave quit his job as a computer programmer at United Airlines and went all in on their burgeoning company.

The Clouses built their business by building trust with their fellow vacation homeowners. Their generosity and friendliness toward their peers resulted in their tiny website, Vacation

Rentals by Owner ("VRBO"), growing into the largest vacation rental site of its era.

As the company began to grow, Dave and Lynn stumbled into a new problem. As rival vacation rental websites began to emerge, homeowners struggled to keep accurate information on all their listing sites. So the Clouses invited ten competitors to a meeting to discuss the problem. Six of them showed up, and four of the rivals ended up launching Renters.org, a free online booking calendar and guestbook that allowed property owners to enter that information once.

Over the next five years, the leaders of these four companies met twice a year at a vacation rental property (of course!) to discuss ways they could better collaborate and solve problems together.

"It was quite an interesting experience working with our competitors," Dave said.[16] "But, over time, the owners of these companies became close friends."

At its peak under the Clouses' ownership, VRBO employed thirty-five people and hosted sixty-seven thousand vacation rental listings across the world. The Clouses eventually sold their company to HomeAway.[17]

One of the first and largest vacation rental companies, VRBO launched a whole new industry with its rival-friendly business model. Today, tens of millions of people vacation differently. Companies like VRBO, HomeAway, and AirBnB are household names.

Mondavi, Mackey, and the Clouses understood the power of *thinking beyond*. Their philosophy is different from simply *thinking big*. Building great companies animated these industry pioneers, but building something beyond their organizational boundaries animated them far more. They each have modeled openhanded leadership and cast a grander vision.

Still, they've maintained organizational boundaries appropriately. Mondavi used his name on his winery's bottles. Mackey didn't partner with *all* his rivals in the food industry. The Clouses eventually charged homeowners to publish listings on their site. But they each led with open hands, humility, and an attitude of abundance.

We believe the time is ripe for followers of Jesus to act with even greater openhanded generosity.

Kingdom Vision

The provocative question Christian leaders need to ask ourselves is this: Are we more animated about building our little clans or about building the Kingdom of God?

Mondavi could have kept his secrets, and the world would have missed out on Napa wine. Mackey could have struck out on his own, and we might think less about the impact of our food on our bodies and our planet. The Clouses could have pursued a strategy only to help themselves, and vacation homes would still be a niche industry. Yet they all understood a bigger mission—something grander than just their own profitability and fame.

"Don't believe in kings, believe in the Kingdom," penned Chance the Rapper.[18] Indeed, our churches and organizations seem far too willing to become smitten with petty kings and their castles rather than *the* King and His Kingdom. As we look inside ourselves and survey our peers, we're not convinced Christian nonprofit leaders act with nearly as much courage and creativity as this winemaker, grocer, and web developer.

Yet how much more powerful is our shared mission than Napa Valley's? Delicious wine is nothing compared with knowing the One who turned water into wine. How much more common should collaboration be among people committed to the Great Commission than among rival grocers committed to healthy food? How much more motivation should people who are going to be neighbors for eternity have compared with neighboring vacation rental owners in Colorado?

Wind at Our Backs

To effectively capture a Kingdom mission and not just tout our organizational agendas, Christian leaders need to better understand the amazing work God is doing through all of us together.

Christian faith-based organizations play an enormous role in alleviating suffering and advancing the common good in our world today. This is not based on conjecture but on research done both here and abroad. Where Christian faith-based organizations abound, communities flourish.

For example, in American cities where there are more faith-based homeless shelters, there is a smaller homeless population.[19] In American cities, the average church contributes approximately $150,000 of social services to their communities annually.[20] Forty percent of the top fifty American charities are faith-based.[21] Across all sectors, churches and faith-based organizations create $1.2 *trillion* in economic value annually in the United States alone.[22]

Faith-based urban mentoring organizations, Christian schools, pregnancy resource centers, prison ministries, refugee settlement agencies, job training organizations, community development organizations, and all sorts of other creative endeavors dot street corners across the country. And when disasters hit, it is often Christians who lead the response. According to the Federal Emergency Management Agency (FEMA), 80 percent of hurricane and other disaster recovery happens because of nonprofits. And 75 percent of the nonprofits doing the recovery work are faith-based.[23]

But the effect beyond our borders is perhaps even more striking.

Over a dozen studies confirm that countries in which "Protestant missionaries had a significant presence in the past are on average more economically developed today, with comparatively better health, lower infant mortality, lower corruption, greater literacy, and higher educational attainment (especially for women)."[24] In many African nations today, the World Health Organization estimates that faith-based organizations provide 30 to 70 percent of health care services.[25]

"In an age where there's a growing belief that religion is not a positive for American society, adding up the numbers is a tangible reminder of the impact of religion," said Dr. Brian Grim, scholar at the Religious Liberty Project at Georgetown University. "Every single day individuals and organizations of faith quietly serve their communities as part of religious congregations, faith-based charities, and businesses inspired by religion."[26]

From leading initiatives on clean water, Bible translation, job creation, and literacy to fighting human trafficking and hunger, Christians respond to material, spiritual, and social needs in communities around the world. God is at work among His people. And this remarkable work God does gives our neighbors a glimpse of the surprising nature of God's Kingdom.

Grander Mission, Greater Impact

We're writing a book on the importance of openhanded, generous leadership, but we acutely feel the gravitational pull toward self-preoccupation. When we wake up in the morning and go to work, our vision rarely extends beyond the walls of our own organization. There are urgent issues clamoring for our attention, looming deadlines, fundraising constraints, and a variety of organizational challenges.

Our hope is that this book might encourage and equip us all to keep looking up and to keep *seeking first* the Kingdom of God. To choose to serve with open hands instead of clenched fists and be reminded that "our mission" is so much greater than "my mission." To inspire a good kind of FOMO (fear of missing out) by challenging us to "think more deeply about what we might be missing out on in the greater story God is weaving together."[27] The beauty and joy of what God is doing through us working together is far more compelling to the world around us than anything we can do alone.

As Christian faith-based nonprofit leaders, we want to more enthusiastically root for our rivals both because of our unity in Christ and our belief in the Kingdom of God. And we never want to forget that we serve a God of abundance.

REFLECTION QUESTIONS

1. How can you *think beyond* instead of just *thinking big*?
2. What could your cause and God's Kingdom gain if you were to reimagine your rivals as allies?
3. How can you practically make space to look up from your own pursuits to focus on broader Kingdom efforts?

CHAPTER 3

Abundance over Scarcity

When I (Peter) first came to serve at HOPE International, a generous supporter donated several old apartment buildings. These rental properties provided HOPE with a consistent stream of monthly revenue, but the apartments needed regular maintenance, and some were left in disrepair when tenants moved out.

As an organization with a small budget and a thrifty team, we tackled these repairs ourselves during evenings and weekends, removing dead mice or the occasional decaying bird, drying flooded basements, filling potholes in driveways, and prying half-melted M&M'S from radiators.

This work was not glamorous, but we rolled up our sleeves and labored alongside one another, sharing the triumph of freshly painted walls and clean radiators. Funds we saved by doing the repairs ourselves meant we would be able to serve more families internationally. *Esprit de corps* grew as everyone from directors to entry-level staff worked together as equals on this common goal of making these apartments habitable.

These rentals became HOPE legend, and long after they were sold, stories about our time as property managers regularly resurface as warm memories of the "early days." We were *all in* and we did whatever it took to get the job done. Working alongside each other brought a spirit of camaraderie, akin to that of athletes or, in some small way, war veterans.

When I joined the nonprofit sector, this *esprit de corps* was how I envisioned all our work. Chalk it up to youthful idealism, but I imagined hard work, compelling missions, and formidable challenges forging an uncommon unity. And not just unity within an organization but unity within an entire sector. With the serious needs of our world, I envisioned a team of people figuratively rolling up their sleeves and working together. I assumed backbiting and ruthless competition were exclusive to Wall Street banks, far away from the noble nonprofit.

I was wrong.

In a *New York Times* op-ed, David Brooks wrote of thick and thin organizations, an idea borrowed from James Davison Hunter and Ryan Olson of the University of Virginia. "A thick institution is not one that people use instrumentally, to get a degree or to earn a salary. A thick institution becomes part of a person's identity and engages the whole person: head, hands, heart and soul," he wrote. "Thick organizations think in terms of virtue and vice. They take advantage of people's desire to do good and arouse their higher longings. . . . People are members so they can collectively serve the same higher good. . . . In [thick institutions] there's an intimacy and identity borne out of common love."[1]

As I joined a Christ-centered nonprofit and spent evenings and weekends working on rental properties, I imagined this sector as home to the ultimate "thick institutions." We collectively serve and love the same God. We collectively face formidable obstacles and know that there is too much work for any one person or organization to accomplish alone. And best of all, we believe we are united in Christ for all eternity.

While there are certainly moments of "thickness" as Brooks describes, the decades we've spent in nonprofit service have opened our eyes to a less altruistic picture of the nonprofit sector. We've observed nonprofit leaders, charities, and churches exhibit posturing instead of partnership, competition instead of collaboration, and organizational agendas instead of a Kingdom cause. Occasionally, there are glimmers of hope—and we will profile how these organizations embody "thickness" in the remainder of this book—but they remain only glimmers.

Chris and I don't just see these negative attributes in others; we have too often seen them when we look in the mirror and consider our own attitudes and actions.

At our best, we are openhanded and generous, empowering other leaders to succeed and celebrating their wins. At our worst, we are prideful and tight-fisted, internally rooting against rival organizations, resenting their success with hypocrisy dripping from our lips as we speak of our desire to expand Christ's Kingdom. In these moments, we act like we serve a very small God.

Many Christian nonprofit leaders know we could be doing more together than we can alone but struggle to become more generous, openhanded leaders. Something is holding us back, stifling our impact.

Two Core Questions

Eager to learn about how to more fully root for our rivals, we sought respected leaders in a variety of sectors who model radical openhandedness. We called and emailed asking them for their perspective on collaboration, and unsurprisingly, they shared freely.

We invested time listening to and learning from these organizations. They were diverse. Some were prominent institutions like Compassion, Life.Church, and International Justice Mission. Others like Esperanza International, Max7, ReadySetGO, Invest-Credit, and Center for Community Transformation were less well-known but just as creative in modeling a posture of openhandedness.

We wanted to explore what they *believe*, and what they *do*, and in some small way, emulate their example of generous leadership. As we learned from these leaders, we saw that their posture and practice seemed to hinge on their answers to two central questions:

1. Do we live in a world of scarcity or abundance?
2. Are we focused on our clan or the Kingdom?

Consistently, we heard these uncommonly generous leaders share how they believe in a world of abundance and focus their efforts on Kingdom advancement. Their perspective stands in stark contrast to much of the nonprofit world.

Exclusive Rights

In preparation for a large Christian conference, we were thrilled about launching a new virtual reality experience. Our team had traveled to Malawi to capture video footage of a savings group and had composed a compelling experience: it was the closest thing to actually being in Malawi. The conference seemed like the perfect place to debut the new technology, which would transport ministry leaders through a headset into the context where they would see the work done through local churches. We signed the contract, paid the sponsorship fee, and prepared for the launch. We trained our staff. We purchased extra Samsung headsets. We polished the VR experience. Our staff grew excited to share what God was doing through local churches in Malawi. However, just weeks before the conference, we received a surprising email: the conference organizers were breaking the contract. They wrote that we wouldn't be able to share the virtual reality experience.

Especially after all the preparation and the signed sponsorship agreement, we wondered why the conference had made this last-minute decision. Why would they prevent us from sharing this experience with conference attendees?

The response shocked us.

We learned that another Christian organization had created a similar virtual reality experience focused on another part of the world. They agreed to sponsor the conference at the highest level but with one clear request: they wanted to be the only organization providing a virtual reality experience.

They wanted exclusive rights.

While this might be a common approach in corporate sponsorships, this stipulation seemed out of place at a conference designed to encourage and inspire Christian leaders. At the core was the idea that there is a limited audience and that having another virtual reality experience might decrease the focus on this organization. They believed there wasn't enough attention to go around.

In the middle of this experience, a board member said to me (Peter), "It's just a business deal." These words were meant to calm my ruffled feathers and encourage me not to take the decision personally. I appreciated the sentiment but disagreed with his basic premise. When we treat one another as competitors, a "win" for our organization is more than offset by a loss for the Kingdom! Exclusivity flows from the idea that we live in a limited world. That there isn't enough for us all, so you need to protect what's "yours." Old Testament scholar Walter Brueggemann writes, "The central problem of our lives is that we are torn apart by the conflict between our attraction to the good news of God's abundance and the power of our belief in scarcity—a belief that makes us greedy, mean and unneighborly."[2]

In this powerful tug-of-war, we found openhanded leaders always lean toward the good news of God's abundance. The God who created the universe is big enough to trust with our daily organizational issues. Great Christian nonprofit leaders refuse to see through a lens of scarcity, and the result is a far greater impact for us all.

Abundant Justice

"In light of the global need, we are always going to feel like we only have five loaves and two fish," reflects Melissa Russell, senior vice president of Global Advancement at International Justice Mission.[3] Russell shared how every ambitious nonprofit leader will feel the almost-constant pang of constrained resources.

No matter the organization's size, it's easy to feel as if we don't have enough. There is always more work to do and bigger dreams to pursue.

If there was any place you would expect a scarcity mindset, it would be in fundraising. In a literal sense, if another organization receives a donation, doesn't that mean that there is less for you? It can feel like flying standby on an airline: there are a limited number of seats, and if someone else gets that last seat, you're stuck in the terminal waiting for the next plane.

This is what makes Russell's leadership at IJM so uncommon. She leads their global fundraising efforts yet rejects the scarcity mindset. She holds a worldview where five loaves and two fish are always enough.

Not much is known about the little boy with the basket of five loaves and two fish who gave his lunch to Jesus, but we do know his paltry amount of food seemed just about ridiculous in the face of five thousand hungry stomachs. When the disciple Andrew noticed the little boy and his basket, he said to Jesus, "There is a boy here who has five barley loaves and two fish, but what are they for so many?"[4] Andrew clearly doubted that Jesus could use something so small. But Andrew was mistaken. God takes a basket of five loaves and two fish and turns it into a massive meal, with plenty of leftovers.

Too often, all we see is our little baskets instead of the One who created the fish.

Russell believes that the God who created the universe is not resource-constrained. We serve a God who created plants to bear fruit and animals to multiply,[5] grew His family through a woman known to be barren,[6] showed His power by raining bread upon His people,[7] and multiplied loaves and fish to feed multitudes.[8] "If everything belongs to the Lord, then there is no scarcity of resources," reflected Russell. "We offer whatever we have to God and watch how God does 'immeasurably more than all we ask or imagine.'"[9]

When we lead from a posture of scarcity, we fight for a bigger piece of the pie. We see others as competition, feeling challenged and threatened by the success of our rivals. If we lead from a posture of abundance, we are free to celebrate one another's wins.

Russell faced this choice in 2014, when the Amyotrophic Lateral Sclerosis ("ALS") Association experienced a momentous breakthrough with the Ice Bucket Challenge campaign. The idea spread like wildfire. Social media lit up as everyone from high school algebra teachers to Bill Gates participated in this creative way to raise funds to fight against this disease.

But then some pushback arose. Some began to wonder if, considering other global crises, so many resources should be dedicated to fighting a disease affecting relatively few people. Someone even made an infographic to portray how much money is raised for respective diseases versus how likely they are to kill us.[10] During The ALS Association's record-breaking fundraising and awareness-building success, a well-meaning supporter reached out to Russell and commented, "I wish all of this ice bucket challenge attention was for IJM."

"But I'm excited for them!" responded Russell. "Imagine the impact this funding might have on families struggling with ALS." There was no hint of envy—only celebration as she cheered on this other organization. "You can be free to fully celebrate others when you believe there is no scarcity of resources," she summarized.

Russell models what we heard from other openhanded leaders: when you look at the world through a lens of abundance, you find freedom from toxic comparison and rivalry.

The average American household gives 2 *percent* of their net income to charitable causes.[11] Fiercely competing over 2 percent isn't our only—or our best—option. People won't give more because we argue why our organization deserves a greater share than our peers of that 2 percent. We believe people will give more as we show how our world will improve if they give 3 or 4 or 10 percent instead of 2. Instead of arguing among ourselves for a tiny sliver of 2 percent, let's join together to argue for increased generosity that will open the floodgates of compassion, justice, and grace.

While the first core belief deals with *how* we see the world, the second deals with *who* is in our focus.

Clans vs. Kingdom

The second core worldview question relates to the parameters we set and how broadly we define "our people."

> **CLAN:** everything and everyone inside our organization's boundaries.

In one of the most well-known but perhaps least-practiced parables, Jesus explicitly expands the parameters of our love. The story begins when an expert in the law attempts to test Jesus. "Teacher," he asks, "what shall I do to inherit eternal life?"[12]

Jesus responds with a question of his own. After the expert correctly answers that our faith can best be summarized by loving God and loving our neighbor, he wants to go one step further in justifying himself. So he asks Jesus, "And who is my neighbor?"[13]

He wanted to understand the parameters of love. When he asked, "Who is my neighbor?" he was asking a dangerously deceitful question. As Palestinian pastor Rev. Dr. Munther Isaac shared, he was trying to eliminate responsibility for others by making some people "non-neighbors."[14]

He wanted to understand who was "in the circle" and who was out. Whom did he have to love? By extension, whom could he justify *not loving*?

It's a question we ask today—whom do we really have to love and serve? Who is on "our team"? Do we love those in other organizations, or can we stop at the end of the org chart? Do we love those near us or do we really have to care about people far away? Do we have to love those who drive a different color buggy or come from a different ethnicity? How about different social classes? Different races? Different political persuasions?

We want to know the parameters of love. Who is in our circle and who is out?

Beyond These Walls

Far from granting the expert permission to love and serve only his nearest and dearest, Jesus responds with the parable of the Good Samaritan, an oxymoron for His listeners who thought of Samaritans as villains, not heroes.

In the parable, Jesus doesn't go into the motivations of the priest or the Levite who bypass a beaten and bleeding man. We don't know if they were busy or distracted or willfully negligent of the need, but the cause doesn't seem to matter.

Perhaps our neglect of neighbor isn't willful, but we wonder if it matters. If a "rival" organization is in need, what is our responsibility? Or what if those we serve—in need of justice or opportunity or the good news of God's love—could be better served through collaborative efforts? What does God ask of us? All too often, our focus is limited to our walls, rarely extending our vision beyond our organizational boundaries. But we believe there is an opportunity not just to build a small clan but to participate in building the Kingdom of God. In the book *Churches Partnering Together,* authors Chris Bruno and Matt Dirks note, "Active, gospel-centered partnership is marked by one driving passion: the kingdom."[15]

> **KINGDOM:** where we submit our efforts to God's reigning authority and become co-laborers in a shared mission to bring heaven to earth.

Jim Tyson, pastor of City Church York in York, Pennsylvania, is focused on the Kingdom, not his clan. Rather than pouring limited resources and capacity into church-branded programs, Tyson's gaze is outward. Living and serving in York, Pennsylvania, he is active in one of the most violent cities in the state.[16] Working solo with his church, his impact would be limited, but Tyson is a Kingdom-focused leader committed to collaboration. "From my perspective," shared Tyson, "I don't need to create some new organization or committee to address the needs of our city. We just need to find the people who are already doing great work and join them!"[17]

Tyson continued, "If we really want to be here and be the Church, then we need to learn how to be the Church together. There are a lot of us who believe that the Church's mission is not contained within its four walls."

Tyson's approach is to identify who is already doing good work, forge creative partnerships, and then determine how he and his congregation can join their efforts. This includes local schools, children and youth services, neighboring churches, government organizations, police officers, and anyone working to bring hope to the city.

"People are productively serving, not reinventing wheels," shared Tyson. He knows that so much more can be accomplished when a variety of people and churches are willing to join together, without caring who gets the credit.

Tyson's approach flows from a belief that he's not building his "clan" but rather he is part of building the Kingdom of God. You won't see his church's name on any of the programs or approaches, but you will see members of City Church actively serving throughout York.

While Tyson's approach accomplishes more, it is uncommon. It requires humility for this church to say their brand doesn't need to be on every program and approach. A focus on Christ and the Kingdom of God helps remove our need for recognition and allows us to accomplish so much more. The unity of the body of Christ, the surprising nature of God's Kingdom, and the abundance of the Creator we worship provide a theological foundation for rooting for our rivals. But how exactly do we do that?

To think through these issues, we needed a better framework for considering how generous Christian leaders like Jim Tyson see and respond to the world around them. Mapping this out in a simple two-by-two helped bring clarity both to what great leaders do and what holds us back from doing it more.

Abundance + Kingdom

What distinguishes generous, openhanded leaders is how they answer these two worldview questions, "Do we believe in a world of scarcity or abundance?" and "Is our focus on our clan or the Kingdom?" These questions change the way we look at the world and directly impact the way we serve.

Plotting these two questions on a simple two-by-two, we see that leaders tend to be drawn into one of four categories.

Some (quadrant I) are so consumed with striving to meet their own needs—real or imagined—that they fail to acknowledge the Kingdom beyond their cause. Others (quadrant II) are aware of the Kingdom and perceptive of the needs around them, but they cannot escape the fear that there isn't enough. Still others (quadrant III) fail to grasp the extent of God's Kingdom and grow apathetic or cynical toward other organizations.

As we interviewed and observed leaders (openhanded and otherwise), we came to realize that there is no partial credit on this two-by-two. One quadrant alone—Kingdom-minded,

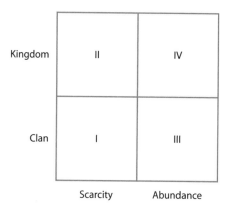

abundance-perceiving leaders—will be equipped to root for their rivals in the unity Christ enjoins.

We aspire to inhabit the upper-right quadrant and become generous and openhanded leaders. But there is a gap between knowing where we want to be and actually getting there. We know ourselves well enough to notice attitudes and behaviors that are subtly pulling us away. To have any hope of leading well, we first need to identify what ails us. And this is where an ancient list helps us understand our maladies.

REFLECTION QUESTIONS

1. Are you prone to perceive scarcity or abundance? How do circumstances affect your outlook?
2. Do you treat interactions with others in the nonprofit sector as "just a business deal" or as opportunities to build the Kingdom?
3. Can you think of a time when God made "five loaves and two fish" enough?
4. What would it look like for you to focus on the Kingdom, not just your clan?

PART TWO

HOW WE ROOT FOR RIVALS

CHAPTER 4

Seven Vices vs. Seven Virtues

During the launch of a new economic development program in Rwanda, HOPE International Country Director Rev. Erisa Mutabazi led a devotional on Exodus 4:2. In this verse, God, after listening to Moses' doubts, asked, "What is that in your hand?" God then used Moses, with the staff he held in his hand, to lead the greatest rescue in history, freeing a band of slaves from the infinitely more powerful Egyptian Pharaoh.

"God often uses what His people already have in their hands to work in miraculous ways," Erisa shared. Erisa continued with the stories of a widow whose last drops of oil God multiplied to save her sons from slavery;[1] David, who killed Goliath with a slingshot and stone;[2] and Jesus, who fed five thousand with a boy's five loaves of bread and two fish.[3]

"Imagine what would happen if a movement of Christ-followers used the gifts God has given to bring healing to a broken world!" he challenged our staff in Rwanda. Imagine if we all freely used what was in our hands in service to Christ.

Wanting Reverend Mutabazi's words to reach our staff, friends, and partners around the world, we captured his message on video.⁴ We hoped it would encourage all of us to use what we've been given to serve God and others.

After launching the video, the first feedback wasn't at all what we expected. It was a voicemail from another organization with a very clear request to stop using this video. The reason? They shared that they had trademarked the question God asks Moses in Exodus 4:2, "What's in your hands?"

For some time, I (Peter) sat in stunned silence. You can trademark a Bible verse? I didn't even think that was possible! Doesn't God hold the copyright?

This was an organization I deeply respect, but this was a request I didn't understand. In a subsequent conversation with the president, I learned of his concern that two organizations using a similar message in their advocacy might lead to confusion among supporters. I also learned that they hadn't received a trademark on the verse (turns out that isn't possible) but rather had filed for a trademark. While I understood the desire for distinctiveness, attempting to trademark God's Word for proprietary marketing privileges seemed unusual.

A few months after comfortably justifying my righteous indignation, a marketing piece from a third organization came across my desk. On the front page they, too, had used Exodus 4:2. "What!?! They are using *our verse!*" I snapped. *How dare they! That was our video! That was our message!*

I began preparing a "cease and desist" email that outlined my grievances when Chris gently pointed out the enormous log protruding from my eye. Funny how effortlessly we spot issues in others while overlooking them in ourselves.

What causes us to so easily stumble into a heart posture where we call our lawyers instead of celebrating our shared mission?

What causes us to think that something (especially a Bible verse!) is ours, instead of holding everything with open hands? It often begins with a faulty idea of ownership.

Unhealthy Ownership

As a man who knew something about kingdoms, we think King David would have understood our struggles. In David's forty-year reign over Israel, the Hebrews finally defeated their enemies, the Philistines, and through his victories, David united the tribes of Israel. The Bible calls David a man after God's own heart,[5] yet one of his most prominent stumbles occurred when he became enraptured by his kingdom rather than *the* Kingdom.

The ensuing suffering of the nation of Israel shows this transgression was no minor mishap in God's eyes.

In 2 Samuel 24, Samuel shares the story of David's census of Israel. David orders his army commander, Joab, to carry out a census over the entire nation. While Joab is a loyal soldier, he recognizes the motive behind David's order. Joab is bold enough to advise David against ordering the census, but David pays no attention. He was king. He disregarded Joab's critique and went ahead with his census.

Why was Joab so concerned about this seemingly benign census? In Israel's culture at that time, you only had the right to take account of what belonged to you. David was taking ownership of the Israelites, claiming them as his people. He was confusing stewardship with ownership. In response to David's decision, God brings judgment through a terrible plague.

God gave David much, but as we tend to do, David forgot that it was all a gift. He forgot that his father, Jesse, hadn't even presented him as an option to Samuel as a candidate for king.[6] He forgot how he was clearly chosen by God and how "the

Spirit of the Lord rushed upon [him] from that day forward."[7]
David was given a position and the Spirit to lead, but over time,
he forgot that these were gifts.

David slipped into the unhealthy assumption that somehow
he "owned" Israel. That he deserved to know how many people
were in *his kingdom*. David's false idea of ownership—rooted
in the vice of pride—was an affront to God. He focused on his
clan and temporarily lost sight of the Kingdom.

Whether it's "owning" a verse or thinking "our" organization
is somehow superior, this same spirit plagues Christ-centered
organizations today. God gives, and, all too quickly, we claim
ownership.

How can we remember that everything we have is a gift?

Knowing vs. Doing

Nonprofit leaders united in Christ should be exemplary partners and colleagues. We don't need more examples like Robert
Mondavi (the "father" of Napa Valley) or John Mackey (the
founder of Whole Foods) to know this is the right approach.
Our shared love and devotion to Jesus Christ and desire to serve
God by serving "the least of these"[8] is enough common ground
for us to actively collaborate and cooperate.

In talking with friends and colleagues, there is widespread
agreement that there is too little Kingdom collaboration. As we
wrote this book, we asked leaders a simple question: "Which
word—collaboration or competition—better describes the current relationship between Christian nonprofits?" Competition
was the clear winner.

Even though we are firmly convinced of our need to give
generously and collaborate radically, we have much room for
improvement in applying these principles. What inhibits us?

As we looked to Scripture, drew from our own experiences, learned from others, and delved into the realms of psychology, sociology, and church history, it became clear our rivalry with one another is rooted in pride and its unsightly offshoots. To understand how we could better root for our rivals, we needed to better understand the sin permeating our hearts and our organizations.

Even if we agree on *why* we should root for rivals, moving into *how* we do that will require we think about virtue and vice. Virtues are the positive habits of the heart that shape us as individuals and our institutions. But we need to understand what ails us before we can apply these antidotes. The good /bad news is our problem is as old as the human condition, and it was clearly articulated and codified over sixteen hundred years ago.

The Birth of the Deadly Sins

The Seven Deadly Sins originated with a group of Greek theologians known as the desert fathers. While they certainly weren't the first to commit them, they gave us a name for the pervasive sins that persistently drive a wedge between us and God, fracture our relationships with one another, and stifle openhanded generosity.

Evagrius of Pontus (346–399 AD), the first to enumerate the sins, noted the vices as gluttony, lust, avarice (greed), sadness, vengeance, sloth, vainglory, and pride. In the late sixth century, Pope Gregory the Great reduced the list of eight to seven, combining sadness and sloth into one, adding envy, and distinguishing pride as the root. He then ranked each sin's severity by the degree to which it offended against love. Thomas Aquinas elaborated on the list in the thirteenth century, identifying the sins as vainglory, envy, sloth, avarice, wrath, lust, and gluttony, with pride again serving as the root.

Today we know these offenses as the Seven Deadly Sins, but they were originally called the Seven Capital Vices. Capital, in this context, implies a source or fountainhead: a vice that leads to others. Rebecca Konyndyk DeYoung has written extensively on the vices, and we have leaned heavily on her work. As she writes, "Vices concern deeply rooted patterns in our character, patterns broader than a single act but narrower than our sinful human condition in general."[9]

There's something to be said for the staying power of these Capital Vices. After hundreds of years, the list still regularly turns up, both within faith communities and the broader culture. The resurgence of the centuries-old Enneagram, which bases its personality types on these Seven Deadly Sins, has brought recent attention to this ancient list.[10]

The Seven Deadly Sins show up in pop culture too. Some have speculated that Winnie the Pooh, Charlie and the Chocolate Factory, and Gilligan's Island all based their characters on the Seven Deadly Sins, and there's no question what inspired the popular Japanese manga-turned-Netflix series *The Seven Deadly Sins* and the 1995 blockbuster thriller *Seven*. You can take an online quiz to determine which deadly sin you are guilty of, based on telling facts like your dream car and your Ryan Gosling movie of choice (feel free to ask us which one we are!).[11] Though the quiz's merits are dubious, in some form or another, each one of us wrestles with these vices.

As we wrote this book, the Seven Deadly Sins offered a helpful and sensible framework. It doesn't take more than a quick glance at the daily news to attest how this list withstands the test of time. These seven sins plague us, endanger the health of our institutions, and inhibit openhanded generosity. By naming these sins in the context of faith-based nonprofit leadership, it's our hope we can better prevent and address them.

Loving Out of Order

Augustine, a contemporary of Evagrius, is perhaps the most important theologian in church history. The North African philosopher was one of the first and clearest to articulate the complexities of sin and grace and vice and virtue. In his *Confessions*, he describes with blunt honesty how these vices haunted him throughout his life.

> But they were like things muttering behind my back
> And like things stealthily plucking at me to make me look
> back.[12]
>
> St. Augustine

He goes on to describe sin as "disordered" loves—a concept no less apt now than in the fourth century. "The person who lives a just and holy life . . . has ordered his love, so that he does not love what it is wrong to love, or fail to love what should be loved, or love too much what should be loved less (or love too little what should be loved more), or love two things equally if one of them should be loved either less or more than the other, or love things either more or less if they should be loved equally."[13]

That is to say, our love of food should not be stronger than our desire to see that all are fed. Our ambition to grow an organization must not lead us to disparage fellow organizations. Our passion for our cause should not result in organizational arrogance or anger with those engaging the problem differently. And, above all, our love for God should not be eclipsed by any other love.

In Augustinian philosophy, what makes the vices dangerously alluring is that they are just slight distortions of genuinely good things: growth for our organization, security for our staff, recognition for our causes. These good things, pursued "in the wrong way, at the wrong times and wrong places, too intensely, or at the expense of other things of greater value," lead to sin.[14]

In *Purgatorio*, written in the fourteenth century, Dante builds upon Augustine's idea of sin arising from disordered loves, categorizing the vices as stemming from misdirected, deficient, or excessive love. We found this framework helpful for understanding how charities, churches, and leaders relate to one another. To the degree that our love is misdirected, deficient, or excessive, our leadership will be distorted, undermining our collective impact.

Returning to our two-by-two, we see virtue or vice arise from the reciprocal relationship between the order (or disorder) of our loves and our answers to the two fundamental worldview questions: Is there enough? Is our primary focus our clan or the Kingdom?

	Scarcity	Abundance
Kingdom	II Misdirected (envy, vengeance)	IV Generous
Clan	I Excessive (greed, gluttony, lust)	III Deficient (sloth)

Twisted Love

In *Rooting for Rivals*, we will use this framework to unpack how these vices plague faith-based nonprofit leaders and, by extension, our organizations. You could argue about the specific placement of the vices in the two-by-two, but we found this overall framework helpful in diagnosing the underlying perspectives and sinful patterns that make us less generous and less focused on our grander mission. Our disordered loves and the ensuing vices fuel an undercurrent that pulls us away from a generous posture where we are able to root for rivals.

As the "root" vice from which all the others grow, pride results in misdirected, excessive, and deficient love and does not appear on our two-by-two. Chapter 5 considers how the vice of pride infiltrates our organizations, urging us to preserve ourselves at the expense of a unified mission.

Quadrant I: Excessive Love (Scarcity + Clan)

Excessive love hardly sounds like a bad thing, but as Dante conceived of it, there is such a thing as too much love for ourselves. We fall prey to the excessive love vices—greed, gluttony, and lust—when our concern for ourselves and our clan comes at the expense of others. Like Pharaoh in the Old Testament, we fear a coming famine, and we hasten to create a monopoly on scarce resources—whether tangible or intangible—ensuring there will be enough for us, regardless of the impact on others.[15] The excessive love vices are driven by our perception of scarcity—irrespective of reality—combined with myopia, insecurity, or narcissism that result in our inability to care about a Kingdom beyond our borders. Excessive love of self or clan causes us to grab as much as we can for ourselves, ignoring needs or opportunities beyond us.

While we often think of the vices on a personal level, the organizational applicability is clear. Chapters 6 through 8 unpack the manifestations of excessive love in our nonprofits, such as our belief that satisfaction is found in possessing more (greed), our insatiable appetite for growth (gluttony), and our willingness to use people for our purposes (lust).

Quadrant II: Misdirected Love (Scarcity + Kingdom)

A Kingdom mindset invites us to look beyond our organization's boundaries. Ideally, we see the success of other organizations and celebrate the ways God is working through them. But misdirected love warps our vision. The powerful grip of perceived scarcity keeps us from celebrating Kingdom wins. Instead we see what others have and imagine that it could have, or should have, been ours. The results are envy and vengeance, vices we explore in chapters 9 and 10. Envy is evidenced in craving what God has given to others and triggers discontent with our own circumstances. Our desire for vengeance, sometimes overt and other times simmering below the surface, is seen in rivalries and dissension among co-laborers in the Kingdom.

Quadrant III: Deficient Love (Abundance + Clan)

When we don't *need* to ask God to provide our daily bread, it is easy to simply ignore our need for God. In places of abundance, we are tempted to miss the beauty and the power of God's Kingdom. Quadrant III leaders believe everything begins and ends with them. They see themselves as the ones who must generate the results. It's too heavy a burden to bear for inherently limited people designed to function as a part—not the whole—of God's bigger plan. The striving of those who perceive abundance yet overlook the Kingdom becomes hopeless and defeating. By God's design, we were meant to function as people of a united Kingdom rather than disparate clans. Quadrant III's clan focus leads to despairing apathy (sloth), which we examine in chapter 11.

The seven deadly sins draw us away from quadrant IV and toward ourselves. To counteract these vices, we'll contrast each with a corresponding virtue. Although there have been attempts throughout church history to pair each vice with a virtue, these attempts have lacked the staying power or cohesion of the vices. As a result, we've chosen—somewhat arbitrarily, we'll admit—a combination of virtues outlined in these previous lists, all rooted in Scripture. These virtues offer a path to resist and subvert the power the vices exert on us individually and organizationally and shape us into more generous and openhanded leaders.

Quadrant IV: Loving Generously (Abundance + Kingdom)

Quadrant IV (generous love) is driven by an others-focused, abundance mentality. It is where leaders and organizations have the greatest Kingdom impact. It's where we celebrate the success of others, believing the world is not one of scarcity. It's where there are grander visions extending beyond an organization's walls.

To arrive in this quadrant requires intentionality in overcoming the vices with corresponding virtues. To counter pride with humility. To choose contentment instead of envy. To invite grace to overcome vengeance. To discover generosity as the antidote to greed. To practice temperance to defeat gluttony. To counter lust with love. And to become steadfast instead of slothful.

Bible translation would seem a likely place for this type of generous love and openhanded collaboration. Getting all of Scripture into every language is a clear goal shared by the global

Church and many organizations. But like every sector, it's also a place of fragmentation.

In fact, one foundation executive in Tennessee shared how one year, three different agencies approached him for funding to translate the Bible into the *same language* for the *same people group*.[16] Literally, the impact was going to be a third of what it could have been if each organization focused on a different language. This type of redundancy is all too common within the nonprofit sector.

But a new example of generous Kingdom partnership is emerging.

Many translation agencies have looked up from their own efforts to realize their organization-centric pursuits were thwarting the collective mission of eradicating Bible poverty in our generation and making disciples of all nations. Together with humility and openhandedness, they focused on a shared mission of translating the Scriptures into every remaining language in the world.

Mart Green, founder of Mardel Christian & Education and chairman of the Hobby Lobby board, was perhaps the first to articulate a broader vision. In both professional and philanthropic pursuits, Green was committed to helping more people access the Bible. He reasoned that rather than having Scripture translations housed in separate systems within the various translation agencies, organizations and unreached populations alike would be better served by a digital Bible library, accessible to all. He brought together three translation agencies and several significant philanthropists to mobilize this vision. The library launched in 2010 and now encompasses more than eleven hundred Scripture portions and versions.[17]

Meanwhile, Todd Peterson, chairman emeritus and interim CEO at the time of Seed Company (a Wycliffe Bible Translators affiliate), was focused on the organization's mission to see all languages have Scripture by 2025. To do so, he was beginning to communicate to supporters not simply the needs of Seed Company but rather the greater needs of the remaining Bibleless people groups. Captivated by the larger vision, donors gave more generously than Seed Company had ever seen before. The organization shared this outcome with Green and then invited other translation agencies to collaborate on how best to invite donors to give to ensure every tribe and every nation would get Scripture in their heart language in our lifetime. They contended givers might allocate greater funds to an overall area of interest rather than a specific organization.

It was a radical idea, as collaborative fundraising usually experiences strong headwinds, and donor events are not typically the place to find organizations praising their "competitors." But with an attitude of abundance and an unwavering focus on the Kingdom, Seed Company viewed these other organizations as allies. They invited others in, and those invited came.

Individual agencies surrendered exclusivity and competition. "It means that you're trying to make someone else successful," said David Wills, president emeritus of the National Christian Foundation. "Our primary responsibility is to not get in the way of what God is doing."[18]

In 2017 ten Bible translation agencies, involved in more than ninety percent of global translation work, banded together to drive visitors to a single website titled illumiNations.bible. In just one visit to the site, supporters can see Bible translation progress across the globe and be matched to translation projects based on interest rather than organization. This collaboration enables the Bible to be translated with better quality, efficiency, and affordability.

Leaders of these ten distinct translation organizations agree that the goal of growing their organization's reputation is subservient to the goal of making Christ known. Rather than compete for website visits or donors, these agencies have pooled their resources to accelerate their goal, accomplishing faster what would have taken vastly more time and resources to achieve independently. Knowing they needed to build relationships, they committed to meeting every month in person in Dallas. Bible translators initially predicted that they would begin translation into the last language by 2150, but by working collaboratively, illumiNations believes they will have translated "at least the New Testament for 99.9 percent of the world's population by 2033."[19] Through translation partnership, they plan to reach their goal over one hundred years ahead of the initial timeline.

In this beautiful example of rooting for "rivals," Peterson and other Bible translation leaders who once competed for market share have allied against their common enemy of Bible poverty. In joining together, they have learned to say, "Thy kingdom come" instead of "my kingdom come."

It's a far more compelling mission, with a far greater impact. They have achieved this by attacking the vice that rules all other vices. To collaborate on such a compelling project across ten different organizational boundaries, these leaders first needed to kill their pride.

REFLECTION QUESTIONS

1. What keeps you from holding what you steward with open hands?
2. How do you see disordered loves at work within your own organization?

3. How does fragmentation in your sector lead to unnecessary redundancy?

4. What is one change you could make today, whether through partnering or eliminating redundancy, that would help another organization in service to the Kingdom?

Pride vs. Humility

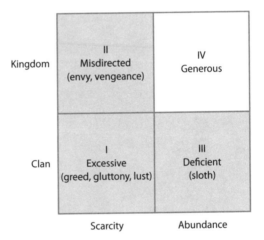

	Scarcity	Abundance
Kingdom	II Misdirected (envy, vengeance)	IV Generous
Clan	I Excessive (greed, gluttony, lust)	III Deficient (sloth)

W hat is more important than saving the world?" Shimon Peres, then president of Israel, asked Shai Agassi.

Nothing, Agassi decided. So in early 2007, Agassi launched Better Place to do just that.

"There has not been a car since the Ford Model T that has been sold at one hundred thousand volume driving on anything other than gasoline," Agassi proclaimed at the 2009 Frankfurt Motor Show. His new company, Better Place, would be a "new beginning" for the transportation industry.[1]

His big idea was to create the world's first electric car network—like a mobile network, but for electric cars. From the Davos Economic Forum to the *Charlie Rose Show* to *The Colbert Report*, Agassi made the rounds like many celebrity entrepreneurs, pitching the world his plans to eradicate global dependence upon oil.

The crowd for his TED Talk erupted in a standing ovation after Agassi's inspirational address.[2] In his TED Talk and elsewhere, he went so far as to compare the launch of his company to the decision to end the slave trade two hundred years ago.

New York Times columnist Thomas Friedman predicted Agassi was the next Steve Jobs[3] and the mastermind of a forthcoming "energy revolution."[4]

"You don't count on the wind to carry you," Agassi said. "Make your own wind and bring about change."[5]

Investors lined up behind Agassi's vision. In just a few years, Better Place raised almost $1 billion.[6]

"I think it's one of those seminal companies that is going to change the way the world operates," Alan Sussman, Silicon Valley venture capitalist and Better Place investor, told CBS.[7]

Fast Company named Agassi to their Most Creative People in Business list in 2009.[8] Agassi promised to sell one hundred thousand electric cars and to launch networks of electric car charging stations in Israel, Denmark, Hawaii, and Australia. World leaders rallied around him.

"We believe this is the future," said Gavin Newsom, then mayor of San Francisco and now lieutenant governor of California. "We say, 'Prove us wrong; don't assume us wrong.' We believe in this."[9]

"This is the infrastructure project of our generation," Agassi predicted.[10]

There was just one problem: the world-changing electric car company needed to sell cars in order to build their revolutionary electric car network. Over the life of the company, they sold just one thousand vehicles, many to friends and staff members of the company. In 2013, the company went bankrupt and liquidated its assets. Better Place became one of the most dramatic business failures of our generation.

How had the world's most powerful investors, journalists, and politicians missed by so much?

Hallowed Hubris

"Every bit of advice I gave him was wrong. Fortunately, he ignored all of it. . . . I've been wrong throughout," confessed Chris Anderson, then editor of *Wired* magazine.[11]

In December 2008, before the colossal implosion of Better Place, Anderson shared this *mea culpa*. Anderson admitted he *initially* thought Agassi's vision was not feasible: that his dream was a farce. But at the time of this public interview, he was a believer. Agassi had persuaded even his most prominent skeptic. "You're not just reinventing the grid, reinventing the car, reinventing renewable energy," Anderson opined, "you're also creating the biggest lithium ion battery consumer on the planet by a factor of five to ten?"

Agassi didn't deny it. He had confidence he was the man to do it. Agassi was set on fulfilling Shimon Peres's prophecy that he would save the world. He would not just reinvent cars, nor the power grid, but the entire way the world thought about energy.

In an interview with Charlie Rose, Agassi opened by establishing his credibility.[12] Agassi described how he built a $100 million software company that was a subsidiary of a "fruit company," with his tongue firmly in his cheek. He was referring to Apple, of course. Apple eventually broke ties with Agassi's company because, as he said, Apple's leaders failed to see his vision.

"They kicked me out in '96," Agassi said. "I worked on . . . a technology [they said] would never pick up," Agassi stopped to roll his eyes at Apple's folly. "It was called Internet browsers."

Shai Agassi looks the part of a celebrity. Young, confident, and poised, Agassi projects optimism from the stage. Agassi is good-looking and funny, possessing the sort of charisma that makes his Better Place mirage a bit more understandable. When he talks, you have no trouble understanding how he earned audiences with the world's wealthiest and most powerful people.

"He has very high self-esteem," said Idan Ofer (in 2009), one of Better Place's first big investors. "He sees himself as a world-recognized figure."[13]

But his swagger—Agassi's confidence in himself—would become what sunk his dream.

Listening carefully to Agassi's interviews and talks from 2007 through 2011, there is an intoxicating assurance in his claims. *I discovered. I learned. What they did wrong. What they missed. Critics said. The problem with hybrids. The problem with Tesla. The fundamental thing people misunderstand. What we've done. What we'll do differently. As I wrote. I came up with that big question. We are creating a new market. I've learned every industry.*

Agassi speaks in popular parlance. Sweeping promises and bold proclamations. Huge vision and searing critiques of rivals, predecessors, and naysayers alike. From politicians to entrepreneurs to celebrity pastors to Twitter commentators, this language is all too familiar.

Max Chafkin, a journalist with *Fast Company*, wrote the definitive eulogy after Better Place's collapse.[14] He interviewed former staff members, world leaders, investors, and even Agassi himself. And the story the eulogy told was a clear one: Shai Agassi's ego sat at the very center of the company. And of the company's demise.

Lest we are tempted to write off Agassi's example as irrelevant to Christian leaders, it's important to acknowledge how much we share in common with him. Like Agassi, our organizations have noble aims. Like Agassi, we rightly desire to change the world. To solve big problems and rally smart people around us to action. Pride lurks in our hearts just as it does his. Perhaps we share more in common with Agassi and Better Place than we are comfortable admitting.

The Great Sin

"If I am a proud man, then, as long as there is one man in the whole world more powerful, or richer, or cleverer than I, he is my rival and my enemy," wrote C. S. Lewis in *Mere Christianity*.[15]

Pride, according to Lewis, is *the* great sin. It is the vice before, above, and encapsulating all other vices. Pride is the antithesis of humility and the "utmost evil" and the "complete anti-God state of mind."[16]

> **PRIDE:** being consumed with yourself.

In *Purgatorio*, pride is the first and most dangerous terrace of sin Dante describes.[17] John Cassian, one of the developers of the list of Seven Deadly Sins, wrote early in the fifth century that pride "reigns over" the other sins as the "queen of sins." He goes on to say pride is the "root of all evil."[18]

In many of the early iterations of the lists of deadly sins, pride wasn't listed as *one of* the deadly sins but the root from which all other sins grow. Pride stands as the chief reason we have trouble rooting for rivals. Still, few of us think the sin of pride is *our* problem. But our cravings are not so different from Agassi's. We want recognition and awards. We imagine our ideas featured in TED Talks and our writing published, recognized, and commemorated. We desire recognition.

Consider the following questions:

Do you celebrate when your rivals prosper?

Do you ever revel in your rivals' struggles?

Do you like when your work leads to someone else's success?

Do you celebrate if you see other organizations flourishing by using your strategies and model?

How protective are you of your ideas? Of your plans, procedures, and policies?

"All evil began with some attempt at superiority," wrote G. K. Chesterton. "The wickedest work in this world is symbolized . . . by a looking-glass; and it is not done in public-houses, but in the most private of all private houses which is a house of mirrors."[19]

This is why pride is the only vice that doesn't show up explicitly on our two-by-two grid. It's because it is the vice found throughout the grid, as an undercurrent pushing us to think more of ourselves and less of others. It is both toxic and prevalent for faith-based nonprofit leaders. It is everywhere, and it is deadly in its effects not only on organizations where it abounds but also on the nonprofit sector and our culture.[20]

As we've written, this way of thinking developed slowly for us. We are leaders "doing good"; aren't we inoculated from pride? We were self-deprecating and tried to intentionally acknowledge others. We believe our work matters and are pursuing it wholeheartedly. But deep down, we had bought the wares popular leadership gurus were selling. We baptized leadership "best practice" without testing the merits of the counsel. Much of this is good, but some of it is built on ideas about organizational success that contradict what the Bible teaches.

Consider these popular leadership tropes: *build your platform, protect your ideas, pursue your dream, capture the market, follow your passion.*

These philosophies have varying degrees of incongruence with a biblical, cruciform vision of success. For followers of Jesus, our joy comes when others succeed. We thrive when others thrive. We hurt when our rivals hurt. Our platform exists to make God's name great, not our own.

Pride, Lewis writes, "is spiritual cancer: it eats up the very possibility of love, or contentment, or even common sense."[21] Likewise, South African minister Andrew Murray once wrote pride is the "root of every sin and evil" and humility the root of every virtue.[22]

Humble leaders understand their true rivalry has nothing to do with their "competitors" and everything to do with themselves.

The Humble Queen

Scripture beautifully (and painfully) communicates the honest motivations of many of our ancestors. Cain killed his brother because he detested how everyone adored Abel.[23] The disciples fought about who was the greatest among them.[24] And, in perhaps the most powerful warning about the dangers of pride, we read about the men who constructed the Tower of Babel.

The sin at the Tower of Babel is not that humans tried to build something great but rather their motivation for doing so. The leaders cast a compelling vision: "Let us make a name for ourselves,"[25] they said, taking an approach still echoing throughout boardrooms today. Their effort was doomed from the start.

But Scripture also gives us examples of women and men whose motivations eschew the innate human inclination to make our own names great. Perhaps none stand as clear as Esther, who humbly stewarded her leadership as queen of Persia.

> **HUMILITY:** subjecting yourself to a grander mission.

Esther reached the peak of influence and pinnacle of power when she was named queen of the vast empire of Persia. She had every reason to believe in her own greatness. But Esther understood her role was not to make a name for herself but to faithfully obey her God, even though she and her people were a religious minority in Persia. Esther learns of a genocide planned against her people and is faced with a choice: risk everything to do the right thing or ignore the threat. Facing high stakes, Esther embodies courageous leadership.

"Then I will go to the king, though it is against the law," she said, "and if I perish, I perish."[26]

For those who grew up attending Sunday school, it's easy to gloss over these words. But when you put yourself in Esther's royal shoes, the magnitude of this statement becomes clear.

Esther risked her reputation, her status, and her very life—everything—on behalf of the most vulnerable of her people. The king grants her the freedom to express her concerns. And in the company of the man who threatened the lives of her people, Esther speaks truth to power.

"We have been sold," she asserts, "I and my people, to be destroyed, to be killed, and to be annihilated."[27] The king, who knew nothing of the plot, sides with Esther and executes Haman, the genocide's mastermind. Esther's enemy is gone, but her task is not yet complete. She again petitions the king, who grants his permission for Esther and her adoptive father Mordecai to "write as you please with regard to the Jews, in the name of the king, and seal it with the king's ring."[28] Esther and Mordecai craft new legislation, protecting the Jewish people from persecution. And because of Esther's humble leadership, the less powerful around her prospered.

Humble leaders give up what could be theirs on behalf of what is beyond them. Humble leaders often operate quietly, consistently elevating others and the Kingdom above themselves. They are unconcerned with notoriety and disinterested in acclaim.

Evidences of Ego

Inside Better Place, the company looked nothing like the vision Agassi proclaimed from the stage. Agassi's leadership philosophy undergirded the company's culture.

"There was profligacy, marketing problems, hiring problems, problems with every conceivable part of the business," wrote Chafkin about Better Place's demise. "There was questionable oversight by the company's board of directors. There was bad luck. And there was hubris."[29]

In a previous executive leadership role at software giant SAP, Agassi said this about his company's competition with their rival, Microsoft: "We're both going in with swords drawn, and we're going to do battle until we win. And there's not going to be any other result. We'll do everything possible to draw blood."[30]

In a "fixed pie" worldview, there are only winners and losers. There is no other category. Individuals and organizations must decide which they will be. Will they take or cede market share relative to their peers? This hubristic philosophy shows up in all aspects of pride-laden organizations, just like it showed up at Better Place.

"We thought we could do everything better," said a former board member.[31]

From the beginning, Better Place never acted like a startup. They paid huge salaries. They outfitted their lavish headquarters with only the best fixtures. They lambasted cynics and blew off potential partners in the auto industry. Better Place was a company defined by its otherworldly ego.

"It was a beautiful dream to dream; people got hooked. It was only later that you'd see the redundancy, the arrogance," a former employee confessed.[32]

Agassi's predictions may not all be fantasy. Change is coming in the energy and transportation sectors. Agassi's dream was not foolish on its own merits. But Agassi's arrogance inhibited him from ever becoming the man to lead the revolution.

Individual arrogance breeds organizational arrogance. Despite our belief that "God opposes the proud but gives grace to the humble,"[33] pride remains rife in our organizations and approaches.

Peter and I (Chris) have seen this in our own lives. Believing in our model and mission, we've inflated our importance. Like many of our peers, we've suggested our approach is better than others. We've said every other type of good intervention to alleviate poverty comes second to ours or is marred by pitfalls our approach avoids. We wonder how many companies and nonprofits find themselves in a season akin to the 2007–2011 heyday of Better Place.

Companies that celebrate ego and employ narcissists at the helm can seem to prosper while the good guys falter. But short-term indicators can be deceiving, as organizational psychologist Adam Grant found when he researched how over thirty thousand individuals across the world engage with one another.

Grant discovered all people fall into one of three categories. They are givers, takers, or matchers. Matchers make up most of the population and, as the name suggests, mimic the prevailing culture of an organization. Takers are prideful. As Grant describes, they consistently show concern for their own goals and needs above everyone else's. And, according to him, "Takers tend to rise quickly and fall quickly."[34] They achieve quick results, often, but rarely achieve lasting success for themselves or their organizations. On the contrary, "Givers . . . make their organizations better." From a secular standpoint, Grant's work affirms Jesus' two-thousand-year-old promise: "It is more blessed to give than to receive."[35]

Our adherence to Jesus' teachings is not a cosmic quid pro quo, where we follow the words of Scripture as if they were a time-tested business manual and expect to soar past other organizations. Rather it's an expression of our trust in God, and our humble acknowledgment that He has called us to something greater than what a growth chart can measure. "People think faithfulness is equal to fruitfulness," said Chris Gough, director of church engagement at Seattle's Union Gospel Mission. "Fruitfulness, though, comes from the Father. We're called to be faithful."[36]

My Charity > Your Charity

Early in my (Chris's) career, I strutted into a church meeting room and hooked my laptop up to the projector. Soon, dozens of Coloradan business leaders and pastors filled the room. They grabbed bagels and coffee and sat down awaiting my presentation.

I shared the standard HOPE pitch but ended with a fresh finale. The week before, I added a new slide to really seal the deal: HOPE wasn't just great; we were *the greatest of all time.* On the slide was a very simple chart illustrating the superior effectiveness of HOPE International's work compared with our peers. On the chart, I plotted how much it "costs" HOPE and our peers to serve one person per year. Of course, HOPE came out the clear winner in contrast to our peers fighting human trafficking, promoting child sponsorship, and digging wells.

In my memory, and I hope I was more nuanced, my remarks went something like, "As you can see in this chart, HOPE is ten times more effective than these wiener organizations."

When I concluded the presentation, I opened it up for questions. One pastor in the group asked directly, "Don't you think it's a little misleading to compare HOPE to these organizations in this way?"

The question lingered in the room. And in a strange way, it was like his question was a mirror. And what I saw wasn't pretty. Pride lurked just behind the slick PowerPoint slide. It masqueraded as a nonprofit effectiveness comparison. But it did nothing more than chart my ego.

We might not think pride is our problem. But more likely, we are just blind to it.

In our culture, we excuse some forms of peacocking. We expect politicians to flaunt their records. We applaud musicians and athletes who declare their dominance. We "like" when our leaders repost other people saying nice things about themselves.

There's nothing wrong with talking about why we love the work we do. There's nothing wrong with sharing the ways our teammates have innovated, nor the ways God has provided and the lessons we've learned. But there's everything wrong with telling everyone how awesome we are *in comparison to others*, no matter how noble our cause. When we do, there's a very real danger that our love is disordered—that our love for our cause eclipses our love for God. That we're building our organization with more fervor than we're building the Kingdom.

Nonprofit leaders should quantify our impact, assess our work's effectiveness, and invite the critiques of charity evaluators. But, at least during this presentation, I extended incredible generosity to HOPE and our model and virtually no generosity to the organizations I presented as our rivals. As Pastor Greg Holder says, "When you've been sipping from the putrid cocktail of pride, all of life is a competition."[37] Nonprofits regularly employ chest-puffing approaches to tell our organizations' stories. Buying into a standard corporate marketing strategy, we employ an us-against-them approach.

Here is what makes our approach so radically different from everyone else's. What a lot of other organizations miss. What we pioneered. To really solve the problem. Where other attempts fall short.

We've visited enough nonprofit galas, Christian conferences, and organizational websites to know it's commonplace. Nonprofit leaders play nice when we're all in the *same* room, but get us in front of a room of potential philanthropists? Well, we just aren't afraid to tell them about the many ways our approach is superior to our rivals'. We may dress up our pride with really nice words and compelling PowerPoint slides, but it's pride at the core.

We're tired of telling the HOPE story in this way. We have not yet fully eradicated—and we likely never will—pride in our messaging and posture. When we're sitting with philanthropists who go *on and on* about the other organizations they support, we must fight the impulse to interject, "But let us tell you about HOPE. . . ."

To help protect us against ourselves, we've instituted practices on our fundraising team to help us grow in humility. We set the goal that each of our fundraisers would recommend a "rival" ministry to HOPE donors at least quarterly. We also set "Kingdom culture" goals largely focused around serving other ministries by helping *them* to raise money.

If virtually every theologian who has studied Scripture and studied the human heart is wrong, then we probably have nothing to worry about. But if they're right, the vice of pride plagues us and it impairs our Kingdom vision. It may not be blatant. It may not be flashy. But if we search our hearts and our organizations, it's there. Sometimes it shows up in presentations. Sometimes it shows up in an unwillingness to ask for help. Other times it shows up in insidious humblebrags. Overt or veiled, we can be confident pride lurks inside us and in our organizations.

It's easy to look at leaders like Shai Agassi and organizations like Better Place and critique the pride we see permeating the presentations, decisions, and strategy. But it's much harder to look at our own hearts and organizations and do the same. To diagnose our pride, we need to start by assuming it is there. And we will only grow humbler by inviting colleagues and critics to help us see our blind spots and learn from those who embody humility.

Humble leaders like Queen Esther offer a blueprint for how to eschew pride and embrace humility. She understood God did not promise she would grow in fame or even experience the fruit of her labor. Queen Esther had no assurance her selflessness would work. But this had little bearing on her decision to do what God had asked her to do.

Practicing Humility

Humility is strengthened when we go out of our way to serve other people and organizations. When Gary Ringger founded Lifesong for Orphans, he took with him the sage advice of his father: "It's amazing what can get done when you don't care about who gets the credit."[38]

Ringger entered the nonprofit sector almost by accident. Out of college he joined his father in the family business, manufacturing and distributing feed. The successful company soon expanded to wholesale food distribution, but despite the family's experience in a related industry, the new business struggled. Gary felt the weight of a failing business. After several years, he was considering giving up on the business when he decided to make a deal with God. If God would enable the company to be successful and give Gary the opportunity to sell it, the proceeds would go to Kingdom causes. In 2002 that opportunity came.

Friends encouraged the Ringgers not only to give their money but also to invest themselves in a cause they were passionate about. Gary and his wife, Marla, had joyfully partnered with friends raising funds to grow their family through adoption, and they found God drawing them to the idea of helping orphans as they waited for or transitioned to their forever homes. The Ringgers set up a family foundation to fund the nonprofit, but Gary was convicted. "It was as though God was saying, 'You have spiritual pride about your family foundation. It's not about your family, it's about *my* family. This ministry is not yours. It's mine.'"[39]

As Gary grew Lifesong for Orphans, he looked for ways to build an organization that supported and served the Kingdom, not just fulfilled its singular mission. From his business background, Gary understood the value of shared services. He came alongside other nonprofits and offered to provide their back-office support. It was a generous, Kingdom-driven offer since Lifesong's work on their behalf is indispensable but virtually invisible.

Lifesong currently provides services like accounting and IT for eighteen organizations that maintain their own identities and branding. These organizations are able to put more funds to Kingdom use rather than overhead because they don't have to replicate Lifesong's infrastructure. "Our impact is far greater when we have the goal of the Kingdom instead of trying to do something great for ourselves," Gary shares.[40]

To fight the root vice of pride, humble leaders:

1. **Dignify those they lead.** "If you want to know what a man's like," said Sirius Black in the *Harry Potter* series, "take a good look at how he treats his inferiors, not his equals."[41] In Adam Grant's research for his book *Give and Take: Why Helping Others Drives Our Success*, he found just that. Prideful leaders "have a history of kissing up and kicking down. They treat those above them exceptionally and those below them like dirt," Grant said.[42] "Narcissists and people with big egos are almost always the most confident and appear warm and engaging at first . . . [and] they often describe success in terms of 'I' and 'me' and not 'we' and 'us.'" Humble leaders acknowledge their inner narcissist and wake up each day warring against it.

2. **Articulate their limited capacity.** Better Place failed because their leaders believed more highly of themselves than they should have. What they modeled went beyond enthusiasm for their idea and a desire to persevere through challenges (which serve entrepreneurs and leaders well!) to a hubris-laden failure to learn, grow, and recalibrate. They believed their mission was destined to succeed and their aspirations would undoubtedly be actualized. In so doing, they failed to embrace their limitedness. They refused to believe their tale might not have a happy ending. For followers of Christ, we need to be comfortable knowing many of our endeavors may not be deemed successful through the eyes of the public. We might fall short of our goals or fail to accomplish our dreams. But again and again through Scripture, God's concern is with our faithfulness, not our performance.

3. **Publish a failure report.** Nonprofits feel the pressure to communicate only the good news, often glossing over the hard realities, mistakes, and shortcomings all nonprofits encounter. That's what makes a "failure report" like the one published annually by Engineers Without Borders Canada even more powerful.[43] Rather than brooding on their challenges internally, they publish them externally. The Denver Institute for Faith and Work followed a similar path in 2017 when they published their annual report with the theme "Pain in our work." In the report, staff members, volunteers, and constituents shared vulnerably about the personal sin and organizational challenges they faced over the previous twelve months.[44]

4. **Value others' work.** Gun violence in Chicago was spiraling out of control in 2016 when a group of leaders in the

city met to explore the question, "Is there more that can be done to address the root causes of the current level of violence we are experiencing?"[45] As they embarked upon a six-month research phase, the group, which came to be called Together Chicago, discovered many others who had long been working to combat the problem in their own unique ways. They formed a coalition under the banner "One City. One Mission." Working with churches, educational institutes, law enforcement, business leaders, and nonprofits, they seek not to replicate what is already being done but to unite the efforts of these groups to address the root causes of violence in the city. They admit there is much work remaining to be done, but Together Chicago celebrates that the number of homicides in Chicago dropped 16 percent from 2016 to 2017.[46] Humbly acknowledging our limitations allows us to ask the same question of the problems our nonprofits seek to address: What partners could help us explore and implement upstream solutions?

5. **Chase after the mission beyond the mission.** It's not unusual to find colleges boasting anything from athletics to academics, clubs to campus culture. But Fuller Theological Seminary is different. In fact, the entire "About Fuller" page on their website is dedicated to the "mission beyond the mission." Recognizing themselves as disciples of Christ before Christian educators, leaders of Fuller see educational ministry as only a small piece of a much larger mission to serve Christ and His Kingdom. "The components of this mission beyond the mission are not options for us," their website reads. "They are abiding imperatives, grounded in the divine command and reinforced by the needs of our times."[47] Not only does Fuller see how its own

mission fits into the Great Commission, but the seminary doesn't lose sight of the grander mission in pursuit of its own.

REFLECTION QUESTIONS

1. What drives you to succeed? Are these motivations driven by building a name for yourself or glorifying God?
2. Who are the people in your life who can help you recognize your own blind spots when it comes to pride?
3. Do you more readily admit your own failures and limitations or point them out in others? Are you willing to really listen to constructive criticism or do you immediately dismiss it as inaccurate or irrelevant?
4. Have you ever rooted for another organization's failure? Why?
5. How do you regularly remind yourself of your grander mission?

////// **CHAPTER 6** //////

Greed vs. Generosity

	Scarcity	Abundance
Kingdom	II Misdirected (envy, vengeance)	IV Generous
Clan	I Excessive (greed, gluttony, lust)	III Deficient (sloth)

When I (Peter) fell in love, I fell hard.

While in college, I met a spunky girl with an obvious love of life and a vibrant faith. Our families knew each other, yet we had met on only a few occasions (though each one was etched in my memory). Three years post-graduation, we met again, this time in East Africa where I was working for a microfinance institution and she was teaching third grade in a Rwandan school. We had our first date rafting down the Nile River on August 17. Not a bad first date! We were engaged on October 3 and married three months later on December 30.

There has never been any doubt that she was to be my life-long and adventurous partner—but we weren't given much of an opportunity to bask in newlywed bliss. Shortly after our wedding, I entered one of the most difficult seasons of my life.

While Laurel and I were in the U.S. for our wedding, several staff members at the microfinance institution where I worked conspired to create "ghost banks," stealing thousands of dollars from the nonprofit. They bypassed the system of checks and balances via collusion between the accounting department, the management information department, the loan officer supervisor, and two loan officers. The scheme required collusion on all four levels for the fraud to succeed.

I considered each of these staff members close friends. We had regularly worked, played, and prayed together.

In shock, I wondered, *How could my friends do this?* Even more disheartening was the fact that they were essentially stealing from the families we were trying to help escape crushing poverty.

After seeking confidential counsel from a Rwandan lawyer and the technical unit that oversaw our microfinance work, we developed an action plan and moved swiftly. When the employees arrived at work, we sequestered each staff member to avoid additional conspiracy. Along with our lawyer and two senior staff members, I met with each of the involved staff members. At the end of an excruciating day, all those involved confessed to their collusion and signed their resignation letters and legally binding agreements to repay the stolen funds.

Personally and organizationally, it was devastating.

›GREED: believing satisfaction is found in possessing more.

Rebecca Konyndyk DeYoung writes in *Glittering Vices* that "when [greed] gets one in its grip, the excessive desire to possess trumps even the most fundamental demands of justice."[1] It's not just in international settings where greed shows up. Closer to home, Wells Fargo recently fired 5,300 employees for creating phony accounts.[2] Greed is not location dependent. It happens in Uganda and the United States. In Bujumbura and in Boston. It's also not income dependent—it happens in poverty and it happens in prosperity. It happens in the private sector and in nonprofits. It happens because we all want more.

In exploring fraud globally and domestically, it almost always starts with a small dose of greed. We take "just a little," without realizing that our appetites are seldom satisfied. Mark Heath, partner at the accounting firm McKonly & Asbury, shared, "When it comes to fraud, there's always a pattern of small-scale stealing for years. Almost inevitably, there is a point where greed takes over and fraud expands exponentially."[3]

Once greed has us firmly in its grasp, there is no such thing as enough. DeYoung writes, "The greedy are excessive in acquiring and keeping possessions even to the point of depriving others of what they deserve or need. Greed causes callousness toward those in want."[4]

Greed is often rooted in the worry that there simply isn't enough. It breeds within us an imperative for more. It is the first of the three excessive love vices (quadrant I): vices spawned by a dangerous combination of both a scarcity and clan-focused perspective. The excessive love vices—greed, lust, and gluttony—arise from a protective and insular mindset. They reflect our love, which should be directed toward God and others, back to ourselves, blinding us to the needs of those around us.

Scripture is full of examples of people seizing the good gifts of God and closing their grip around them. This is where greed begins.

Bigger Barns

Luke 12:16–21 recounts the parable of the Rich Fool. Few of us would seek Rich Fool as our enduring moniker, but we can identify with his struggle.

> The land of a rich man produced plentifully, and he thought to himself, "What shall I do, for I have nowhere to store my crops?" And he said, "I will do this: I will tear down my barns and build larger ones, and there I will store all my grain and my goods." And I will say to my soul, "Soul, you have ample goods laid up for many years; relax, eat, drink and be merry."
> But God said to him, "Fool! This night your soul is required of you, and the things you have prepared, whose will they be?"
> So is the one who lays up treasure for himself and is not rich toward God.

Here is a man who wanted to make sure he had enough. In the previous chapter of Luke, Jesus taught His disciples to pray for "daily bread."[5] It's a sentiment echoed throughout Scripture. In Exodus, manna fell from heaven six days a week as the Israelites wandered in the wilderness. They were to avoid the temptation of greed (and they sometimes did) by collecting just enough for the day, with God providing for the Sabbath as well.[6] God's people were to rely on Him for their sustenance each and every day. Trust was built as He continually provided. Proverbs 30 records the wise words of Agur, "Give me neither poverty nor riches; feed me with the food that is needful for me, lest I be full and deny you and say, 'Who is the LORD?'"[7]

The rich man seems to have done just that. Forget *daily* bread! He doesn't want to petition the Lord for years! He fails to see his abundant harvest as a gift from God, and he neglects his responsibility to steward this gift for the benefit of others. His definition of *enough* was sadly warped. He saw a scarce world, and so when he was given an abundant harvest, he hoarded it.

Does "Enough" Exist?

Nonprofits struggle with greed, too. And I (Chris) write from firsthand experience. A few years ago a donor, Dan, wrote an exciting year-end email to Peter. I was thrilled when Peter forwarded it on. Dan and his wife had already given generously to HOPE that year, but they had a $15,000 giving surplus available at the end of the year. They were committed to using this money to meet an unmet need that would further God's Kingdom, and they wondered if HOPE had any needs remaining that year. For a fundraiser, emails do not get better than this.

I quickly pulled together some options and emailed Peter about a few projects where we could use Dan's funds in the following year. But Peter pointed out that my response wasn't quite answering Dan's question. Of course we could use the funds *someday*. There are always great opportunities awaiting in the year to come. But Dan's question was whether we had met our core budget needs for *this* year.

Peter and I both knew something I, as a nonprofit fundraiser, was reluctant to admit: it was likely that this year we were going to hit our annual fundraising goal. Because of the generosity of our supporters, we were having a terrific year. But I was hesitant to admit that reality outside of HOPE's walls.

Discussions about *having enough* are uncommon among nonprofit leaders. I've been in many conversations about there *not* being enough. I've talked to leaders who desperately wished they could grow faster and bigger than their current resources allowed. We have also felt that emotion. The scarcity mindset among nonprofit leaders is real: we live in a constant state of belief that we do not have enough.

It's for this reason that when fundraisers from fellow non-profit organizations attend "our" events, we seat them with one another, and often in a far-flung corner of the room. We live with this fear that one of "our" donors might meet someone from another compelling organization. So, we seat all the people from other nonprofits together to ensure no "poaching" can take place. To the fellow nonprofit leaders reading this book, you know what I'm talking about. To philanthropists reading this book, we're sorry. Like the Israelites with the manna, we see the gifts of God as something to hoard, protect, and store up.[8] Greed twists our understanding of these gifts, and we close our fists around what we ought to share.

In 2006 I began working at HOPE as an administrative assistant. That year, fewer than one thousand donors made contributions to HOPE, totaling just under $3.5 million. What's happened since then has been remarkable. God has provided more than we ever thought possible. In recent years, our annual fundraising has exceeded $16 million. But this fact didn't change my gut reaction to Dan's email: *We need more.*

Every nonprofit impulse within me bristled at the prospect of acknowledging to Dan that we had *enough.* Of opening the door for him to potentially decide to give that $15,000 to another organization. *Next year will be a new year,* I thought. *Our economy could stagnate. We hope to expand our budget next year.* . . . Rooted in insecurity, the rationalizations went on.

To be frank, when Dan's email arrived, I yearned for his donation. I knew I could finagle a response to satisfy him and bring the donation to HOPE. But, in the face of my inner debate, Peter challenged me to consider generosity. To consider opening my hands. To relinquish control of something that was never mine to begin with, trusting God to provide for next year's needs next year, rather than being the Rich Fool who "lays up treasure for himself and is not rich toward God."[9]

So Peter responded with a simple sentence acknowledging our reality. "We could certainly put additional investment to good use in serving more families," he wrote. "However, I did want you to know that it looks likely we will hit our core fundraising target this year, in case there is another organization with a greater need."

I shared this story with a friend who has given generously to faith-based nonprofits for over four decades. He responded that he'd not once experienced a nonprofit say they had enough. I don't write this to pat HOPE on the back, but just to show how provocative Peter's suggestion to consider generosity truly was. This friend's reaction proved just how entrenched the scarcity mindset is among nonprofit leaders and how eager we are to secure more for our clan, even when others in the Kingdom have greater needs. Faith-based nonprofit leaders have a greed problem.

How do we get to a position where we gratefully acknowledge that there's enough? That we can trust God to provide everything we need? What if we actually believed the words of missionary Hudson Taylor that "God's work done in God's way will never lack God's supplies"?[10]

We believe we are invited to practice radical generosity.

> **GENEROSITY:** trusting God's provision and using all we have to bless others.

In Matthew 18, Jesus tells a story of a servant who experienced incredible generosity from his king. The man owed a debt he could never repay, but the king took pity on the man and cancelled the debt. In this parable, we are the debtor, saved only through a generous gift we can never repay. As the apostle Paul reminds us, "What do you have that you did not receive?"[11]

For leaders of Christ-centered nonprofits, this is true on many levels. First, as the parable illustrates, we are people who have been saved by grace, an undeserved gift from God. Additionally, we know that we are able to do our work because generous people have given generously. People don't send donations for us to hoard but to use in serving people. Literally everything we have is a gift. We owe our lives and livelihoods alike to the generosity of God and others. How can we, in turn, not live as radically generous people?

Yet too often we have been tempted to behave as the ungrateful servant in Jesus' story. He left the king's presence as a recipient of tremendous generosity, but he turned around and withheld generosity from a fellow servant in need.

During HOPE's history, we have been blessed by the generosity of openhanded leaders and organizations. When I (Peter) joined HOPE after graduate school, we needed an employee manual. Actually we needed quite a lot—we had maxed out our credit line at the bank, were understaffed, and lacked the experience we needed to thrive. Not knowing where to start, I reached out to other organizations and former employers asking if they would be willing to share. The response was as generous as it was swift.

Here you go—please feel free to copy whatever would be helpful!

So copy I did. Our first employee manual was simply the manual of another organization with their name "found and replaced" with our own. In thirty seconds, we were an official organization with an employee manual.

When we were in the beginning stages of launching a savings group ministry, the Chalmers Center provided the initial trainings and invited us to freely use their curriculum. I (Chris) remember my early months as a twenty-two-year-old Human Resources manager at HOPE. Jennifer Helmuth, the Human Resources director at Mennonite Economic Development Associates, provided regular support as I navigated the complexities of benefits administration and hiring law. She took my calls and emails with grace and shared her time and expertise when I needed it most.

It made no logical sense for these organizations and individuals to help us. They could have used their time to build their own organizations. The vice of greed insists we must focus internally so that we can get more and do more. These leaders instead chose the path of generosity, carving out the time to assist us and sharing their intellectual property to help us get our start. Their generosity may not have contributed to their organization's bottom line, but it was an investment in the Kingdom.

We pray that we will pass on the generosity we have received.

Openhanded Evangelists

Bill "Wink" Winkenbach's family likes to joke that they could have been billionaires.[12] Except they probably aren't joking. Winkenbach and a close cadre of friends are credited with inventing Fantasy Football, the most popular of the fantasy sports experiences that now engage 56.8 million people in the U.S. and Canada.[13] Early on there were discussions of copyrighting the idea.

Andrew Mousalimas, another early pioneer, recounts a long-ago phone conversation documented on Sports on Earth.

Andrew: Hey Wink, I think this will spread. What do you think about copyrighting it?

Wink: Nah, I don't want to.

Andrew: Well, how about me? I'd like to copyright it.

Wink: Over my dead body.

The founders of Fantasy Football were true fanatics. They woke up in the wee hours of the morning to calculate scores, routinely phoned newspapers for more timely intel, and in the pre-Internet world, conducted all of their own research into players. As their own enjoyment of the game grew, they sought to spread the idea, largely by word of mouth. Some even refer to these pioneers as "evangelists" for the cause of Fantasy Football. While they could have copyrighted their idea or charged a fee for their elaborate scoring guide or other intellectual property, they simply loved the game and wanted others to love it too.

Bill Winkenbach, Andrew Mousalimas, and other early converts to Fantasy Football chose generosity over greed. It wasn't for their renown or wealth but rather for what they saw as a greater good for the love of the game—the phenomenon of Fantasy Football.

We imagine the impact if we were at least as passionate in our love and pursuit of advancing God's Kingdom as these men were in furthering the cause of Fantasy Football. Thankfully, we've encountered many examples of this type of openhanded generosity.

Crazy Generous

When Craig and Amy Groeschel founded Life.Church in 1996, it looked like many church plants: forty people meeting in a two-car garage using a borrowed projector and a couple of construction lights.[14] But the trajectory they've taken from there has been stratospheric. As of 2017, Life.Church has locations in eight states with a vibrant Church Online community reaching an estimated 235,000 unique visitors each week.[15]

Early on, Life.Church decided to wholeheartedly embrace the words of Jesus that it's more blessed to give than receive. Rather than desiring more for Life.Church alone, they desired more for the Kingdom. So they've made all the resources they've created available to others for free through their Open Network. On this site, pastors and church leaders can access children's materials, creative resources, tools, ministry ideas, apps, trainings, and community.[16] They decided against selling curriculum and resources and instead actively open-source everything. Generosity is contagious, and today the resources available on Open Network aren't just from Life.Church. They've also partnered with other ministries with the same heart for the local church— like Hillsong, Elevation Church, and North Point Ministries—to offer their resources as well.

They've also created YouVersion, a free Bible app that reached a milestone of 300 million downloads in 2017. Users can find daily devotionals and Bible reading plans, as well as read the Bible in more than sixteen hundred versions and over eleven hundred languages. Wherever we travel in the world, we can share Scripture in the local language through a phone, tablet, or computer.

It's not just large-scale organizations like Life.Church modeling this openhanded posture. Jared Nelms of the Timothy Initiative has a passion for discipleship. After creating curricula titled "Disciples Making Disciples" and implementing it both domestically and internationally, the Timothy Initiative realized their impact could be far greater by sharing it with other organizations. Nelms invites other organizations to "take our training materials, put your logo on it, and use it in whatever way would be most beneficial to you."[17]

We imagine what might happen if the type of radical generosity modeled by Life.Church and the Timothy Initiative were normative. Both operate from a spirit of generosity that prioritizes the Kingdom over their own clan, acknowledging that all they have has been given to them and that God is the source of their abundance. They trust God will provide for their daily needs, even as they generously share with those around them.

Greed starts with a scarce view of the world. Generosity, on the contrary, comes from our confidence in a God of abundance. Battling greed isn't about stifling our ambition for more. It's about redirecting our ambition to a grander vision beyond our own organization's agenda.

Believing God is a God of abundance, generous leaders use their platform for more than just their own causes. Authors talk about their own writing but are generous in promoting the books of others. Nonprofit leaders share about their mission but are generous in highlighting other organizations. Church leaders celebrate the successes of other churches, praying for their health and growth.

Kevin Eshleman, lead pastor of Ephrata Community Church in Pennsylvania, models this type of generosity by actively promoting other churches. While giving announcements during a Sunday morning service, he welcomed visitors and then offered, "We have several really great churches in our community. If our church is not the place where you connect, I'd be glad to talk with you about other congregations in our community that might be a better fit. Please come talk to me after the service if that would be helpful to you, and I'd be glad to tell you more."

We affirm abundance and deny scarcity when we actively praise and advocate for our rivals. When we do, we push back against the vice of greed and "consider how to stir up one another to love and good works."[18]

Practicing Generosity

Our calling extends beyond organizational boundaries. As a result, as we spend time innovating and creating, let's also explore how we can share with others, modeling an open-source attitude.

This is not to say that there isn't a time to trademark, but the question is: What is our default position? Is our initial reaction to be openhanded or close-fisted? Unless there's a compelling reason not to, imagine the impact if we routinely went out of our way to share with others.[19]

Trade secrets and confidential business plans might make sense to maximize profit, but they are not the way to maximize impact. Nonprofits receive favorable tax status because they exist for a public good, not as an end in themselves. If collaboration increases the speed of progress, then we should be the very first to sign up. We exist *because of* generosity. We exist *to exhibit* generosity.

Inspired by the examples of others' generosity, we've created a platform on our website where other nonprofits can freely download documents HOPE has created, ranging from our fundraising philosophy to our employee benefits guide to monitoring and evaluation surveys.[20] We celebrate when we hear that in some small way we've passed on the generosity that we've received. Our strategic plan includes a goal about sharing with others, intentionally tying our organization's success to our openhandedness.

After attending a fundraising event last year, Paul Penley, the director of research at Excellence in Giving, commented: "I have never seen another ministry leader promote and praise other ministries creating jobs for the poor at their own fundraising event!"

What if we all periodically used "our space" to raise awareness and funds for other nonprofits? What if we became the champions of other organizations and not just our own? It's unlikely any nonprofit leader would self-diagnose greed as a threatening vice in their organization, but we've found it lurking in our lives. Intentional generosity is the cure.

To fight the vice of greed, generous leaders:

1. **Open source (almost) everything.** In *The Death and Life of American Cities*—perhaps *the* seminal book on urban planning—author Jane Jacobs writes, "A well-used city street is apt to be a safe street. A deserted city street is apt to be unsafe."[21] Isolated, abandoned, and boarded-up city streets, Jacobs writes, are hotbeds of crime and neglect. The same is true for charities. It's all too easy for us to live in our echo chambers, allowing our organizations to exist solely for ourselves.

   To counteract this tendency, generous leaders like Jordan Steffy let no "street" go unused. Steffy, founder and CEO of Children Deserve a Chance, open-sourced his foundation's strategies and operational plans for the Extraordinary Give. Known as Lancaster County's largest day of giving, the Extraordinary Give stretches donations made to various organizations by at least $500,000. The more an organization raises in those twenty-four hours, the more funds they receive from the "stretch pool." Every year, Steffy and his team spend weeks preparing for this event, developing a "playbook" of initiatives to increase awareness for their cause on this day. Their focus and creativity consistently meant they finished in the top position. As other nonprofits recognized their unique approach and wanted to learn from their example, Steffy generously shared their playbook with others, inviting other organizations to learn from their example and increase their support. He was more concerned with expanding the movement of generosity than fighting for a slightly larger piece of the funding.

2. **Erect standing stones.** Since greed is driven by a fixation on scarcity, focusing on God's provision is a powerful countermeasure. In one of several such instances in the Old Testament, Joshua erects a monument after God stops the waters of the Jordan River, allowing the weary Israelites to cross into the Promised Land.[22] In 1 Samuel 7, God miraculously intervenes to help the Israelites defeat the Philistines. "Then Samuel took a stone and set it up between Mizpah and Shen and called its name Ebenezer [stone of help]; for he said, 'Till now the Lord has helped us.'"[23] Tangible reminders of God's provision are powerful. And they help us recall the ways God has provided "manna" in our organizational lives. When we feel like what we have isn't enough and we're facing the future with fear, reminding ourselves of God's provision helps us to echo the words of Samuel: "Till now the Lord has helped us." Periodically, we turn a wall in HOPE's office into a place to list and remember the prayers we have seen answered and the mountains moved on our behalf. When we find ourselves in a place of scarcity, we find tremendous encouragement in remembering God's abundant provision.

3. **Name drop on behalf of rivals.** Even our speech can reflect generosity or greed. It's easy to be stingy with our praise while unconstrained in our criticism of others. Let's readily celebrate what others do well—mentioning them by name—and, when given the opportunity to draw comparisons between our organization and a "competitor," refuse to speak ill of another organization. One nonprofit leader we know even applies this principle in his speaking engagements, suggesting, "When speaking, leaders of the body of Christ should ask, 'Have I said at least one strong and honest affirmation of an organization that the audience may perceive as a competitor?'"[24]

4. **Proactively serve rival ministries.** In 2009 Elizabeth and Steve Gilroy founded Face of Justice to confront the human trafficking industry in San José, Costa Rica. They created the organization with an openhanded posture in response to the overwhelming needs they observed while traveling in the region. One of the ways they practice generosity is in how they host mission trips. Rather than exclusively introducing volunteer travelers to their work, they always introduce their guests to at least four other organizations. After travelers' week in Costa Rica, Face of Justice staffers provide trip participants the standard nonprofit response cards. But instead of only providing an invitation to support Face of Justice, the cards feature ways they can give to those other organizations as well.[25] Their interns and staff members even go so far as to work on projects for these rival ministries. Rather than expanding as much as they *could* expand, they expand in ways respective of the strengths of their peer ministries in San José.

5. **Create rivals.** Pastor Tim Keller of Redeemer Presbyterian Church is known not just for celebrating rivals but for creating them. During Redeemer's exponential growth, Keller realized that he could best impact his community for Christ by planting other churches in his New York neighborhood. When congregants left Redeemer Presbyterian Church to support other newly planted churches, Keller celebrated their decision. He notes, "Our attitude to new church development is a test of whether our mindset is geared to our own institutional turf or to the overall health and prosperity of the kingdom of God in the city."[26] Since the beginning of his ministry, Keller has helped to plant over four hundred churches in fifty-six cities, sparking a gospel movement in urban regions around the globe.[27]

6. **Impact their communities.** Every November, churches across the nation participate in the Be Rich campaign to partner with nonprofits in their communities and around the world. Since its inception in 2007, the campaign has sparked a movement of outrageous generosity. Participants have donated over $29 million and have volunteered over 272,000 hours of community service in the past ten years. "It's our way of doing corporately what we've all been called to do individually," says Andy Stanley, senior pastor at North Point Ministries.[28] With an emphasis to give, serve, and love, the Be Rich campaign gives back 100 percent of the money raised to support local nonprofits in efforts to better their communities by, among other things, alleviating homelessness, administering disaster relief, and providing clean water.

REFLECTION QUESTIONS

1. Do you believe there is enough?
2. How can you create memorials to remember God's generosity and faithfulness?
3. How can you channel your appetite for more to mean more for the Kingdom, not more for your clan?

CHAPTER 7

Gluttony vs. Temperance

	Scarcity	Abundance
Kingdom	II Misdirected (envy, vengeance)	IV Generous
Clan	I Excessive (greed, gluttony, lust)	III Deficient (sloth)

The moment I learned a Chick-fil-A was opening in my neighborhood is etched in my (Chris's) memory. I'm slightly embarrassed to admit how elated I was.

Since the restaurant's opening a few years ago, my family and I have become regulars. A Chick-fil-A within walking distance is an undeserved gift to my entire family. Plus, any calories you consume at Chick-fil-A are nullified if you walk to the restaurant. Trust me, it's science.

Our neighborhood Chick-fil-A has become a regular haunt for the family. On cold Denver evenings, the playground has faithfully received the pent-up energy of our young kids.

We are big "CFA" fans. My wife and I have completed two opening-day camp-outs and been among the first one hundred customers to grace the floors of a new CFA location, earning us free Chick-fil-A meals each week for a year. One of the camp-outs was in below-freezing temperatures with several inches of snow on the ground.

All that to say, our fanhood of Chick-fil-A's delicious food, legendary customer service, and family-friendly environment runs deep. With the lines regularly running out the door of our neighborhood CFA, it seems curious it took the chain so long to expand into northeast Denver.

But there's a reason Chick-fil-A waited decades to open its first Colorado location. While their competitors surged at impressive growth rates in the second half of the twentieth century, CFA grew at a pace some analysts criticized as unnecessarily slow.

Mark Miller, CFA vice president of high performance leadership shared how Truett Cathy, founder of Chick-fil-A, regularly encouraged CFA management to quit focusing on getting bigger. Instead, he focused on getting better. "Once you get better," Cathy reminded them, "the *customers* will demand you get bigger."[1] Still, critics slammed them for losing potential market share and forgoing millions in potential profits.

Despite a ripe expansion environment, Chick-fil-A's owners capped the company's expansion rate at seventy-five new stores per year. They believed moderating their growth rate would allow them to grow healthier, rather than just growing bigger.

Insatiable Appetite

It may seem strange to open our argument *against* gluttony by arguing *for* an exemplar from the fast-food industry. The irony is not lost on us. Even more ironically, later in this chapter dissecting gluttony, we'll argue for the importance of feasting. As we understand the effects of gluttony on us personally and organizationally, we believe a posture of temperance creates an environment for celebration and appropriate feasting.

Ironies withstanding, Chick-fil-A's radical approach of *purposely stunting their own growth* is one that clashes forcefully with the more-more-more mentality bombarding leaders from all directions. At HOPE, we've regularly lamented our growth in comparison to our flashier and more rapidly growing peers. We've envied their progress, as you'll read in a chapter to come. And, as we've done so, it prompts an uncomfortable question: Do we practice temperance?

All expansion rates feel not fast enough amid a culture tempting us to grow faster and bigger, no matter the costs. This is where Chick-fil-A's example offers a stark challenge.

Historically defined, gluttony is a sin associated with what we eat and drink. In their analyses of gluttony, Augustine, C. S. Lewis, Chaucer, Bunyan, and Dante take aim at just that. But for the purposes of this book, we're exploring the roots of gluttony and the specific ways gluttony plagues leaders of faith-based nonprofits.

> **GLUTTONY:** an insatiable appetite, obsessing over growth and expansion rather than quality and impact.

Gluttony is a close cousin to greed. Like greed, it is an excessive love vice. It exists when faith-based nonprofit leaders hold a scarcity, clan-obsessed outlook. If greed is a warped understanding of God's provision that leads to clenched fists and a "mine" mentality, then gluttony is a warped perception of God's pace and an urgency for "more" at any cost.

A glutton says, "If there is food on the table, I'll consume it now. If there's a bottle in the cabinet, I'll open it now." Gluttons refuse to moderate and refuse to deny themselves, compromising their own health in the process. They always choose indulgence. [2]

Gluttonous leaders believe satisfaction is found in more, now. They are never full and don't trust God's timing. They never have reason to celebrate because they never feel like they have had or done enough. They cannot possibly be openhanded leaders because they cannot possibly imagine letting go of something that could expand their organization.

And this is where the surprising temperance of a chicken sandwich company has something to teach us about gluttony. As leaders, the allure and promise of rapid growth can hold a seductive power over us. A healthy appetite for growth can quickly be replaced by a voracious and destructive appetite for more.

And it's at this point—when our hunger becomes insatiable—that our healthy aspirations for growth become gluttonous.

The Myth of Scarcity

If you've ever taken a stroll around Stanford University, you know the place practically glitters. It's manicured, green, gorgeous, and groomed to perfection. You cannot help but reflect that the ground upon which you are walking has been home to some of the greatest minds of our age. But forget brainpower, these people have serious skills in landscape architecture. If there were ever a shrine to higher education, this place would be it.

This is the work of John Hennessy, Stanford University's most recently retired president, widely considered to be one of the greatest presidents in Stanford's history. Hennessy's impact on Stanford was remarkable. Doubling the university's endowment, Hennessy made way for the Palo Alto campus to expand its interdisciplinary research in bioengineering, bioscience, energy, and computer science, while significantly enhancing financial aid.[3]

In short, Hennessy was a visionary. He contributed in leaps and bounds toward building the Stanford empire.

In an interview with journalist and author Malcolm Gladwell, Gladwell asks Hennessy point-blank, "How much is enough for an institution like Stanford?"[4]

After struggling with the question for a moment, Hennessy responds by saying that because Stanford's ambitions are always growing, so is their need for funding.

Halfway through the interview, Gladwell pushes the issue further.

"Hypothetically, if Bill Gates or Larry Ellison came to you and said, 'I'm giving you $10 billion' . . . would you say, 'We don't need it,' or would you say, 'We could put that money to good use'?"

To quantify a number that large, Gladwell explains that "$10 billion is a few billion more than the gross domestic product of Barbados, and $4 billion shy of the gross domestic product of Jamaica." In order to understand the scope of this question, Gladwell rephrases the question to his podcast audience, "Basically I'm asking, 'What would happen if someone gave you, Stanford, the average economic output of an entire Caribbean country for a year, tax free?'"

Hennessey pauses for a beat. Two beats, to be exact. And then in exactly that amount of time he comes up with a way to spend $10 billion! Mind you, we're not talking about *millions*, but *billions*. "The one area where I think there is opportunity for significant incremental funding is in the biomedical sciences. If that were an endowment . . . I could find a way to spend a half billion dollars a year in biomedical research," said Hennessy.

And just like that, he spent $10 billion.

Finally, Gladwell asks Hennessy if there would ever be a situation where he would tell a funder that their money might go to better use at another institution—if he would ever concede that they have no need for such a large sum of funding. Hennessy's answer, in short, was no.

For faith-based nonprofit leaders, when it comes to funding we're all John Hennessy. We become so consumed with satiating our own hunger that we lose sight of the world beyond our organizational boundaries. Every opportunity becomes one we are best suited to pursue now. Cutting-edge biomedical research needs to be done, more elaborate scholarship programs need to be endowed, and new facilities need to be built. And we are the best ones to do it. This is especially true of visionaries and leaders, who, given their keen ability to foster and facilitate growth, have a hard time recognizing the contributions and capacities of others. But almost inevitably, this appetite for more leads to overexpansion and eventual collapse. As author Jim Collins notes in *How the Mighty Fall*, the undisciplined pursuit of more is one of the key contributors to organizational demise.[5]

Like Hennessy, we are prone to see what *could be* instead of what already *is*. Our eyes glance past what we have and settle on what we want.

The Beauty of Temperance

For Chick-fil-A, a temperance philosophy does not stop with new store expansion. It extends to the hours they open their stores. Their decision to remain closed on Sundays allows their employees to rest, in alignment with the owners' Christian convictions. But consider just how dramatically it affects their short-term bottom line.

If CFA opened on Sundays, it's likely their revenue would grow substantially, at least by 10 to 15 percent. It's a decision that's long confounded industry analysts.

"Last year Chick-fil-A only had about 1,775 U.S. stores to KFC's 4,491," wrote Venessa Wong for Bloomberg News. "Yet in dollar terms the Colonel is coming up short even with that much larger footprint: Chick-fil-A's 2013 sales exceeded its larger rival's by nearly $800 million in the U.S. in 2013. And that's with zero dollars coming in to Chick-fil-A on Sundays, when every restaurant is closed."[6]

When asked about this very dynamic, Dan Cathy, CEO and chairman of Chick-fil-A, said, "On the surface, you'd simply think that Sunday is one of the most popular eating out days of the whole week. So you can kind of make a guesstimate as to how much business we might generate if we were open Sunday. But there are many more underlying elements that are a great benefit that frankly offset the fact that we're closed on Sunday."[7]

Temperance drives leaders to measure the value of long-term benefits against any potential near-term benefits. They are free from the tyranny of short-term goals and able to do what they believe is right. It drives leaders like Cathy to trade opportunities sitting on the proverbial table for better opportunities in the long run. Temperance demands we deny potential good things now in preparation for better things later. And temperance replaces our hunger for more with an abiding satisfaction with what we have.

> **TEMPERANCE:** acknowledging our own limits and celebrating the capacities of our rivals.

Hobby Lobby also operates from this perspective, limiting their evening hours and closing their stores on Sundays and major holidays. Similarly, Hobby Lobby pays their entry-level employees twice the minimum wage, even though they could potentially squeeze more profits from their craft stores by paying their employees less. But the company's leaders believe these constraints create better outcomes for the long-term health of their employees and their company.[8]

Leaders at both companies recognize the fastest pace possible is not always best, no matter the importance of the mission or their unique ability to accomplish it.

Enduring Vision

Frederick Law Olmsted designed and managed the construction of some of the most expansive parks in North America, including Central Park in New York, Golden Gate Park in San Francisco, and Mount Royal Park in Quebec. Citizens and visitors to these fine parks have been appreciating Olmsted's work decades after his death because of Olmsted's commitment to sacrificing quick fixes for enduring, long-term vision. If you asked Olmsted whether you should plant a tree or throw down some mulch, he would almost always argue for the former.

"I have all my life been considering distant effects," wrote Olmsted, "and always sacrificing immediate success and applause to that of the future."[9]

At the foundation of temperance is understanding the limitedness of our life and work. When embracing limits, leaders find freedom, not constraint.

Hungry for Apricots

Years ago, I (Peter) had two simple charts on my wall—one for fundraising revenue and another for the number of families served. By 2010, I wanted HOPE to serve one hundred thousand families and have annual fundraising revenue exceeding $10 million. I had a clear vision of the annual growth rates we'd need in these two categories over the next five years to achieve that goal.

In setting these goals, my thinking was rather simple: Growth is good, so ambitious growth is even better. Besides, $10 million and one hundred thousand families served by 2010 sounded catchy. There wasn't detailed deliberation in setting these goals, but although they were established rather arbitrarily, they quickly became my obsession.

It didn't take long to realize that growing at a measured, incremental pace would not get us to these ambitious targets. So I began to dream of other ways to boost our growth.

On a trip with a group of supporters, I excitedly pitched a new initiative that had the potential to help us reach our goal of one hundred thousand families and $10 million of revenue: apricots in Uzbekistan. Through a connection, I had learned of a partnership opportunity for an apricot farm in the former Soviet Union. It would require a significant investment, but it would create opportunities to serve thousands of families and hopefully raise additional funds.

Mentally, I said yes to this opportunity almost immediately and began exploring ways to raise the funds. I could see the growth charts moving up and to the right and could almost taste the apricots. Did I mention I love apricots?

After my pitch to the group of supporters, Wil, a friend and investor, asked me something that knocked me right out of my apricot trance. "What is the current unmet demand for what you're already doing?" Roughly speaking, at the time, microfinance institutions were at best serving 25 percent of the global market. And Christian organizations were meeting less than 1 percent of the global demand.

His second question was even more pointed, "What expertise does your team have in apricots and farming?" His message was clear: Why would we expand to apricots when there is so much unmet demand for our core mission? What was the compelling reason to expand programmatically? Wil challenged me to remember our organizational limitations and reconsider this type of expansion. His questions forced me to realize I just wanted more.

By God's design we are limited. To the gluttonous leader, these limitations chafe. But temperate leaders know there is beauty in embracing our limits. The truth Wil helped me discover is that gluttonous leadership tendencies will lead our organization astray. Apricots in Uzbekistan wouldn't have been an area of strength for HOPE. Moreover, shimmying our way into the apricot market could very well have taken business away from our "rival" organizations like Partners Worldwide, Sovereign's Capital, and other Christian ministries equipped to serve entrepreneurs with these types of businesses.

In retrospect, my initial response when hearing about an apricot farm should have been, "That's outside our area of expertise, but I would be honored to introduce you to people who are doing terrific work and might be able to help."

Recognizing that others are more qualified for a job requires a modest amount of humility, but it leads to far greater outcomes. What if would-be "competitors" recognized and validated one another's strengths, deferring opportunities to the most qualified player? Imagine the Kingdom impact if this attitude were common.

In time, HOPE grew. Perhaps not at the rate I had hoped when setting my short-sighted goals, but, thanks in large part to Wil's courage in questioning my motivations, our growth was healthy. It did not compromise the quality of our services or the heart of who God has called us to be. We aren't purveyors of fine fruit, but we are honored that God has chosen to work through us—in our limitedness—to impact families around the world.

The Freedom of Limits

Linnea Spransy is an accomplished painter with a master's in fine art from Yale. She's exhibited her work in galleries in Kunming, London, Brooklyn, and many cities in between. Her work features beautiful and striking colors, patterns, and rhythms.

"We actually need our limits. We need our boundedness," Spransy said at a Q Conference talk.[10] "In that boundedness, we can discover great freedom and possibility," she explained.

Great artists understand real freedom cannot exist without limits. "If you want to get things done, you need structure," said rapper and speaker Sho Baraka.[11] This runs athwart gluttony, which promises fulfillment and satisfaction only if we're willing to abandon our limits.

In sports, as in art, creativity abounds not from chaos but within defined boundaries and limits. A pitcher throwing a perfect game or a swimmer setting a world record excites us because of how the athlete performed within the assigned boundaries. A pitcher throws from a defined distance and into a constrained strike zone. A swimmer employs a specific stroke within a standardized lane. It's these moderating rules that make perfect games and world records meaningful. Limits create the conditions within which these performances can be beautiful.[12]

Peter and I (Chris) both have the joy of being fathers. And we know our kids thrive not in the absence of boundaries but within them. We allow our children to prove their readiness for expanded freedoms, rather than granting them full freedom from the start.

When our kids are young, we need to moderate food portions, control the types of foods they receive, and establish regular times throughout the day when they should eat. As our children grow, we increase their freedoms commensurate with their capacity to handle them.

Temperance-minded leaders understand their organizations in the same light. Like great artists, athletes, and parents, they moderate their opportunism, provide boundaries for their team, and offer constraints to create the possibility of real freedom. They recognize that unbridled opportunism is tyranny by a different name. In so doing, they open up opportunities for beautiful partnerships in a way they never could if they tried doing everything on their own. As they regulate their pace, it allows them to recognize and celebrate their organization's limits and others' unique capacities and strengths.

Gluttonous leaders are consumed by their own clans, but this does not mean temperance-minded leaders ignore the good things happening within their organizations. A culture of temperance creates the environment for celebrating successes.

Neither Feasting nor Fasting

Fasting and feasting show up throughout the pages of Scripture, perhaps most clearly in the life of Jesus. He gives clear instructions on fasting in Matthew 6:16–18, and begins, "When you fast . . ." The use of the word *when* instead of *if* makes it clear that Jesus assumes this is a routine part of life. Yet Jesus was also a frequent guest at parties, confounding the religious elite by freely eating, drinking, and celebrating with a motley group of friends.

When asked about fasting, Jesus replies that it's all about timing. "Can the wedding guests mourn as long as the bridegroom is with them? The days will come when the bridegroom is taken away from them, and then they will fast."[13] There is a time for temperance and fasting, and a time for feasting.

When leaders practice gluttony, they seize every opportunity, crave every possibility, and take any ground available to them now. This unsustainable pattern prevents both fasting and feasting, ironically. When every meal is a feast, no meal is. Gluttonous leaders lose not only the ability to say no but also the ability to say yes fully. Because they lack temperance, they lack the ability to really celebrate; there's no time to feast when the next mountain is waiting to be climbed.

God warns His people about the dangers of gluttony, but these warnings do not prohibit, nor diminish the importance of, feasting.[14] On the contrary, a life of temperance creates the possibility of joyful feasting and is vital to the life and ministry of Christians.

In *Keeping Place,* Jen Pollock Michel aptly describes the feast table as "a burning bush." She goes further, writing, "Around the feast we are enflamed with the presence of God."[15]

This burning bush, the feast table, is hidden in plain sight in the Bible. God institutes patterns of feasting in the laws He delivers to His people.[16] Jesus' first miracle takes place at a wedding feast.[17] And the closing pages of Scripture foretell a great, final banquet between Jesus and the Church at the wedding banquet of Christ and His bride.[18]

Feasting in Scripture shows up in a planned and structured way. God's law prescribed seven major feasts God's people were to celebrate each year.[19] Additional feasting appears as a means to celebrate good things like weddings, of course, but also to celebrate other significant milestones, such as when Abraham and Sarah received weary travelers at their home.[20] This is also powerfully modeled in the parable of the Prodigal Son. When the Prodigal Son returns home, his father proclaims, "Bring quickly the best robe, and put it on him, and put a ring on his hand, and shoes on his feet. And bring the fattened calf and kill it, and let us eat and celebrate. For this my son was dead, and is alive again; he was lost, and is found."[21] And they began to celebrate.

The father did not ask his staff to prepare a normal dinner, nor to wrangle up leftovers. He asked them to bring the best clothes and the finest food and to prepare to party. When the Prodigal Son's older brother begins to protest the extravagance, the father will not hear it. No matter the conditions, this reunion demanded a feast. "It was fitting to celebrate and be glad," the father said. "For this your brother was dead, and is alive; he was lost, and is found."[22]

It's interesting we don't know what happens *after* the feast. We don't know if the Prodigal Son actually turned his life around. We don't know if he went on to be a productive member of society. We don't know if he placed his trust in God. We don't know anything about the son's final destination. We just know he reached this major milestone. This moment, though his story wasn't fully written, was worthy of a feast.

Fearing to Feast

For nonprofit leaders, feasting and celebration can feel exorbitant. It can feel almost like gluttony. *Should we really spend donor dollars on parties and celebrations?* It can also feel arrogant. *Are we taking credit for the good gifts God has provided?* It can feel like a waste of time. *We have important work to do—why stop to feast? Think of how much we could do instead of celebrating.* And, perhaps most challenging, it can feel scary to admit things are healthy. *Will donors back off if they know we're thriving?*

But there's a reason feasting shows up so much in the Bible. When done right, feasting amounts to celebrating how God has faithfully provided. Like the Prodigal Son's father, feasting commemorates celebration-worthy moments.

Temperate leaders practice feasting in a lot of ways. They do it literally by throwing parties upon reaching milestones. They bring in breakfast or buy ice cream or throw a party to celebrate key individual, departmental, and organizational achievements. They also feast figuratively. They notice and commemorate achievements whenever given an opportunity to share virtually or in-person with their teams.

At HOPE, one way we've tried to build celebration into our annual rhythms and routines is by elevating the significance of key staff milestones such as five- and ten-year work anniversaries at our annual Christmas party. We also commemorate at our annual leadership summit one staff member, donor, organizational partner, and client who has best lived out our core values that year. We also celebrate staff members for how they live out our values at bi-weekly staff meetings. Our celebration team commemorates birthdays, degrees, weddings, and babies—always looking for moments to thank God. By creating these celebration rhythms, it helps to inculcate feasting into our organizational DNA.

Rebecca Konyndyk DeYoung reminds us that a virtue "is acquired through practice—repeated activity that increases our proficiency at the activity and gradually forms our character."[23]

Practicing temperance and learning how to fast allows us to more fully practice celebration.

Practicing Temperance

Founded by our friends Josh Kwan and Dave Blanchard, Praxis is an innovative organization that exists to equip and resource faith-motivated entrepreneurs "who have committed their lives to cultural and social impact, renewing the spirit of our age one organization at a time."[24]

Rather than aiming to serve all organizations everywhere, Praxis works within very defined constraints: they serve twelve nonprofits and twelve businesses each year. And not just any business or nonprofit. Kwan and Blanchard believe they can add the most value at particular stages of the organization's lifecycle, so they have established specific guidelines around which entrepreneurs will thrive in the Praxis community.

Each year, the number of high-quality applications exceeds the number of available slots. To be candid, more than once Praxis has declined to pursue an opportunity we've proposed to them. Be it new partners they could work with or nominees we think they should consider for the program, we've regularly been denied. At times it's been frustrating. We're mentors with Praxis after all, and wonder why we don't have more sway!

But Praxis is a temperance-practicing organization. Nobody who knows Praxis's team and vision would accuse them of having their sights set too low or of being risk-averse. They're growing and expanding in unique ways each year.

Yet their growth is anything but gluttonous. It's within the boundaries of their vision and is guided by clear constraints. This posture of temperance creates the opportunity for them to invest deeply in the lives of the entrepreneurs, staff members, donors, and investors they serve. One way this manifests is in how they celebrate.

Part of what makes Praxis unique is their "pitch night," when the entrepreneurs share the vision of their organizations. Even in this setting, they're challenging these entrepreneurs to distill their organization into a presentation of five minutes or less. They've seen this constraint generate creativity and punchiness simply not realistic in an hour-long address.

In these pitch sessions, they're sharing their vision with potential high-impact donors and investors. And Praxis appropriately celebrates the courage it takes to do so. Without fail, when the pitch night concludes, the pizza arrives. And the cadre of entrepreneurs and mentors celebrate this key milestone in the Praxis journey. Limiting their cohorts to small groups allows them to really know and be known by each other. And it allows them to truly feast in a way they can't at a massive gathering. This measured pace enables depth otherwise impossible.

Their first mentees began in 2010. Since then, Praxis's fundraising revenue, staff size, and organizational reach have grown steadily.

Leaders like Dave Blanchard and Josh Kwan practice temperance. And they provide an example of how we can too. To fight the vice of gluttony, temperate leaders:

1. **Articulate success.** Temperate leaders understand you can only be satisfied once you articulate a definition of success. Without that, there will never be enough, and success will instead be benchmarked by your most successful peers. Defining success means establishing specific goals, straightforward budgets, and clear expectations for each member of your team. Chick-fil-A exemplified this by capping their growth rate and celebrating when they reached this goal. Rather than always saying yes, they said yes

within boundaries their leaders felt their team and systems could handle.

2. **Celebrate progress.** Gluttonous leaders lose the ability to feast and to fast. By seizing only the right opportunities, temperate leaders know when it's time to party and are able to do so. Praxis throws pizza parties after their entrepreneurs conclude the high-stakes pitch night. The Prodigal Son's father feasted after a key milestone in his son's life. Party when the situation merits it. And schedule parties throughout the year to ritualize the practice of feasting within your organization.

3. **Define their limits.** Establishing a healthy culture of temperance will harness opportunism. Doing so will allow you to recognize where your organizational boundaries end and a rival organization's begin. Then, if an interviewer like Malcolm Gladwell asks for recommendations for other organizations that could help put $10 billion to work, you'll feel the freedom and confidence to share. Rooting for our rivals as a posture means that before expanding into new areas or new approaches, we look to see who is already there. Greg Brenneman, executive chairman of CCMP Capital shared, "Resources for the Kingdom could be multiplied many times by just doing a simple market study of what others are already doing locally, and then making sure that your efforts are complementary to what others are investing in."[25] Focusing on the Kingdom means we celebrate when friends are doing good work, helping to raise awareness and funding for their organizations. It means we actively and intentionally connect and support and don't just initiate. To practice healthy restraint, we need to know ourselves—and our boundaries.

REFLECTION QUESTIONS

1. How do you define "enough" for your organization?
2. How are times of celebration and "feasting" embedded within your organization?
3. What boundaries need to be set within your organization?

CHAPTER 8

Lust vs. Love

	II Misdirected (envy, vengeance)	IV Generous
Kingdom		
Clan	I Excessive (greed, gluttony, lust)	III Deficient (sloth)
	Scarcity	Abundance

Where iss it, where iss it: my Precious, my Precious? It's ours, it is, and we wants it. The thieves, the thieves, the filthy little thieves. Where are they with my Precious? Curse them! We hates them."[1]

Even though I (Peter) was a kid when my dad read the entirety of J.R.R. Tolkien's masterful *The Lord of the Rings* trilogy to our family, I have never forgotten the character Gollum. In my middle school mind, I could see Gollum. Hear his voice. Picture scenes with vivid detail as he debated with his conscience how to get the Ring back in his possession. Stories of the wizards, elves, and hobbits blend together and have lost their clarity, but the story of Gollum is just as clear today as it was when it captivated my imagination years ago.

Gollum stumbles upon a ring offering invisibility, long life, and great power. Immediately Gollum is captured by the promise of the Ring and will do anything to possess it. "We wants it, we needs it. Must have the Precious. They stole it from us. Sneaky little hobbitses."[2]

Over time, however, the Ring corrupts, disfigures, isolates, and controls him. Gollum is sickly and skittish, barely resembling the hobbit he used to be. Imprisoned by his own desire, Gollum allows the Ring and his possession of it to eclipse all that was good in his life. "My Precious!" he calls after the Ring, going to great, horrible lengths to keep it within his grasp. Most painfully, his obsession with the Ring devolves into violence and abuse of the people around him. He wrongs his friends at every turn because he allows the Ring to place a chokehold on his values.

Gollum embodies some of the deepest longings and darkest battles waged within the human heart. His message is so much bigger than a ring. It's a cautionary tale of who we become and how we mistreat those around us when objects or pursuits become our obsession. These passions consume us, and the people closest to us suffer most.

At some level, we all have our own version of "We wants it. We needs it." Little do we recognize that this obsessive pursuit is shaping us. Though we look nothing like Gollum, our obsessions are disfiguring our hearts.

The Hidden Vice

Of the seven deadly sins, lust is the one that seems least applicable to a book on generous leadership. But unfortunately, there's no exemption.

Sitting close together in the quadrant of excessive love, lust, greed, and gluttony share a common thread. Characterized by untamed desire, or an overabundance of love for the wrong things, the vices found in this quadrant can easily run together. Each vice drips of a focus on self and is fueled by the belief that there will never be enough.

Most often, lust's definition is confined to sex. We know the type of indiscretion that has Christian leaders making headlines (and there have been more than enough of these situations to realize it's an issue!), but there's a broader form of lust plaguing faith-based nonprofit leaders. At its root, the vice of lust drives us to objectify people. Lust simmers when leaders abuse their power and take advantage of those around them.

> **LUST:** when we abuse our power by using people for our purposes.

We see this misordered love in Gollum's love of the Ring, which eclipsed all other loves and relationships in his life. His loves were desperately out of order, and his life became twisted as a result. He was willing to do anything to anyone as long as it contributed to him getting or keeping the Ring.

Before his life revolved around the Ring, Gollum was a regular hobbit named Sméagol. In perhaps the most gripping scene in the movie adaptation of Tolkien's story, we watch Sméagol's life transform as he first lays eyes on the Ring during a peaceful fishing outing with his friend Déagol.[3]

Coming across the Ring by accident, Déagol considers the discovery in his hand. Sméagol peers over his friend's shoulders, his eyes filled with yearning as he perceives the Ring's mysterious power. Taken over by an uncontrollable desire for the Ring, Sméagol goes to the greatest length to secure it for himself. He murders his friend, and as he pries the Ring from Déagol's dead fingers, a devilish grin contorts his face—remorse flashing across his eyes for but a moment. Just like that, Sméagol's identity as a free man fades, and Gollum takes his place. Gollum spends his remaining days in isolation, obsessed with keeping the Ring, no matter what that drives him to do.

Gollum provides a picture of lust glaring in all its desperation and depravity. So how do we know if we are allowing lust to slowly disfigure our hearts, pulling us away from health and generosity? It begins with a recognition of how love is the antidote to lust's trap.

Rooting Is Loving

"Lust says, 'What can you do for me?' Love says, 'What can I do for you?'" wrote pastor and author Tim Keller.[4]

At the heart of rooting for rivals is a love of God and love of neighbor. Love is at the heart of rooting. It's not even needing to ask the question, "What's in it for me?" but rather, "How can I show love to you?" To consider the needs of others above our own. To be marked by sacrifice and service, and to regularly go out of our way to care for others with no regard for personal benefit.

If not for alliteration considerations, we could have titled this book *Loving Your Rivals*. Generous leaders start by valuing their neighbors—even those who work at rival organizations—more highly than they value themselves.

> **LOVE:** caring for people in the self-sacrificial, self-denying, others-focused way of Jesus.

In the thirteenth century, Thomas Aquinas wrote, "Love is not only a virtue but the most powerful of the virtues . . . the form of all virtues."[5]

As pride is the root of all vice, love is the root of all virtue. Again and again in Scripture, the virtue of love is elevated above all others.[6] Humility, generosity, temperance, contentment, grace, and steadfastness all find their origin in love.

So how exactly might we better love our rivals?

To fight the vice of lust, we cannot just think our way out of it.[7] We reorder our loves by the practices in which we partake—the daily, weekly, monthly, and yearly practices that form us. It's why we've concluded each chapter with concrete ideas to practice these virtues. Intellectually understanding vices and virtues is a great start, but reordering how we love begins with our practices and habits.

How Lust Isolates

Lust sabotages relationships by objectifying people, and then separates us from community, isolating us from others.

Consider how, even with the broad definition we're employing, publicly admitting a struggle with lust—using people for our own purposes—is perhaps the most difficult vice to own up to. You wouldn't get panicked looks if you confessed struggling with a little pride. You wouldn't hear gasps if you admitted to a little sloth. But admitting a struggle with lust is in a class all its own. So we keep it hidden, pretending it doesn't exist. Like Gollum, we retreat from the very people who could help us find freedom from its grip.

Lust tells us accountability isn't worth the effort. Lust clouds our judgment. It stunts our vision and prevents us from seeing the consequences of our behavior on ourselves and others.

Just as lust poisons relationships, it can be every bit as damaging to organizations. As leaders of Christ-centered nonprofits or churches, our missions are compelling. We are helping people in Jesus' name. We are working to see the Kingdom come on earth as it is in heaven. But so easily, lust twists our hearts, resulting in our objectifying the people around us on behalf of the mission we pursue. The more compelling our mission, the more vigilant we must be in guarding our hearts against the propensity to use people for our purposes. By acknowledging the vice of lust, we admit we can at times love our organization's mission more than we love the people within the mission.

A couple years ago, we contacted a like-minded nonprofit whose work and mission we respect. We had recently benefited from several exchanges with a few other peer organizations and reached out to see if this organization might be interested in a similar meeting. We hoped to share best practices and resources that would enable us and our counterpart to serve our constituents with greater excellence and further our work for God's Kingdom. It wasn't long before a staff member wrote to decline our invitation. Not mincing any words, the reply read, "We don't play well with others."

While some nonprofit organizations don't play well with others, it's rare to hear one blatantly admit as much. This type of thinking marks quadrant I, with its clan focus and scarcity mentality. We understand its appeal, as we've admitted our own tendencies toward greed and gluttony—excessive love vices—in the way we lead. This organization's brief reply suggested a focus limited to their own mission and a perception of scarcity, likely of time, but perhaps also of resources or ideas.

There remains much to admire about this organization, and subsequent conversations with leaders show a desire to address the myth of scarcity and the pull toward self-preoccupation. We believe that reframing their view of abundance and the Kingdom will transform not only their perspective toward outside organizations but also their treatment of those who have dedicated their lives to furthering the organization's mission.

As God leads and guides, may we all learn to "play well with others." The Kingdom will be stronger for it.

A Lustful King

Lust is perhaps nowhere more acutely evidenced than in the life of Ahab, by many measures the worst king in Israel's history. We read Ahab "did evil in the sight of the LORD" and "did more to provoke the Lord, the God of Israel, to anger than all the kings of Israel who were before him."[8]

Throughout his life, he swapped long-term faithfulness for short-term pleasures. He compromised both his values and Israel's to earn the affection of Israel's pagan neighbors. In his first act as king, we read, Ahab marries Jezebel, a pagan queen, and erects an altar in worship to her god. Again and again, Ahab sides with Jezebel and with the practices and beliefs of leaders outside Israel, rather than those appointed by God like Elijah, Elisha, and Obadiah. And Ahab regularly succumbs to his most carnal instincts.

One of the final accounts of Ahab's life is the most pitiful, one typifying Ahab's reign of lustful leadership. In the story, Ahab demands that one of his subjects, Naboth, give him his vineyard. Ahab's reasoning is logical: he is king and he wants Naboth's vineyard for his own purposes.

"Give me your vineyard, that I may have it for a vegetable garden, because it is near my house," demands Ahab. "I will give you a better vineyard for it; or, if it seems good to you, I will give you its value in money."[9]

Ahab's offer to Naboth was reasonable. Ahab's desire for this perfectly located vineyard was not wrong. But lust always perverts a good thing. Like Gollum, he let his desire for what was not his begin to consume him. His passion soon controlled him.

When Naboth refuses to give up the vineyard, Ahab returns "vexed and sullen" and laments the outcome to Jezebel.[10] Jezebel entices Ahab to consider a different strategy for acquiring the land, appealing to his lust, asking him rhetorically, "Do you now govern Israel?"[11]

Translation: use your power to take what you desire, no matter the cost to others.

Because Ahab granted Jezebel his authority, she acts on his behalf, hiring a couple mercenaries to stone Naboth to death. And Ahab gets his precious vineyard. Later, Elijah, with a direct message from God, visits Ahab.

"Thus says the LORD: 'In the place where dogs licked up the blood of Naboth shall dogs lick your own blood. . . . You have sold yourself to do what is evil in the sight of the LORD.'"[12]

Consumed by his desire for Naboth's vineyard, Ahab got what he wanted in the short term but lost it all in the end. He used Naboth to feed his lust, stamping out a life to take what was not his.

Lust always disfigures our hearts and leads to disastrous outcomes. But there is another way to lead.

Finding Joy in the Right Places

James and Carine Ruder loved Peru. Each year, they used their vacation time to take missions trips to visit a small community where they supported an orphanage. When I (Chris) first met James, it was all he talked about. He talked about the children they met there and the ways God was working in that community.

When the topic changed to his company—where he invested fifty-one of the fifty-two weeks each year—his enthusiasm level changed entirely. He and Carine owned and led L&R Pallet, but it was to them just a vehicle to generate profits to give to Peru and to send their family on mission trips. Nothing more.

The mission in Peru continued to thrive. But back home in Denver, things were not going well at L&R Pallet. "I felt like the business had cancer and was dying," said Ruder in an interview with *Conscious Company Magazine*, describing that season at the business.[13]

In the early 2000s, the pallet construction and repair company suffered from a host of woes. The staff and leaders of the company were consumed with intra-staff politics and low morale. The workplace was unsafe, resulting in high levels of workplace injuries. A plant manager blackmailed employees to fund his drug habit. And a handful of staff colluded with a few vendors to embezzle half a million dollars in company profits. All told, people—including the Ruders—just didn't like working at L&R Pallet. And the data showed their displeasure. L&R maintained annual turnover rates above 300 percent.

It was in Peru where James realized he had misplaced affections. While serving in a community there, a young girl touched James's arm and he describes a "God moment" when it felt like electricity rushed through his body.

Through that girl, "God caused me to start *seeing* people rather than simply *looking* at people," James shared.[14] In that moment, James realized that though they were not maliciously mistreating their employees, they were also not truly *seeing*, or loving, them.

Reordered Loves

That moment in Peru began a process of soul-searching for James and Carine, as they sought to lead the company in a way that cared for people. They began to identify how they were shirking their responsibility to love the people around them. Reordering their love meant changing the fundamental ways their company operated. And the process of desiring to care well for his company ultimately led to James caring for and enjoying people more fully than he ever had before.

"I've realized that people who walk by my door are hurting," James said. "There are so many needs here. My responsibility in stewarding the business isn't just to write paychecks. I have a responsibility to shelter them, to lead them, to set an example. I realized I am the only Christian some of these people will ever meet. Where else will these employees go for help when they encounter crises, conflicts, or confusion?"[15]

What transpired over the next few years surpassed even the Ruders' wildest hopes. As they've fallen in love with the mission and people God has entrusted to them, they've been overwhelmed by the possibilities.

Over the course of that time, James has led his company and cared for his staff in a new way. No longer seeing his employees as a means to an end—but as people—has resulted in an entirely new culture. Part of the change has come from James investing in the Burmese refugee community near the plant. Today, over half of his 120 employees hail from Burma. Part of the change has come about because he's discovered the joy of caring for the people right where he is.

"I realized that there is nothing special about being a 'missionary,'" James said. "Right outside my office door, I have my missions field. I want to pour into these people."[16]

Today, turnover is down from 300 percent to 15 percent, which is low for a manufacturing company. James and Carine love their work. Their employees are growing and becoming prosperous. Their revenue continues to increase. And the company has gone from a place of chaos to a place of stability.

When I saw the transformation happening at L&R Pallet, I asked James if I could write a feature on him and his company for the *Denver Post*. He agreed to the interview, but the week before I planned to submit the article, James called me.

"I don't think I want to run the story," Ruder said to me. "I just don't think we're stable enough to go public just yet."

A few weeks later, James called me to reverse his decision. "Run the story," he said.

James shared the real reason he had been nervous about the story gracing the pages of the *Denver Post*. He was nervous about his rivals learning about "his little secret"—the amazing talent pool he had discovered in the local refugee population. He did not want his competitors poaching his employees. Like Gollum and like us, James wanted to protect and clamp down on the new *precious*.

But when he and Carine prayed about it, God reminded them of their role as missionaries. God reminded them of their first love of God and their neighbors. God convicted them to be a voice for the voiceless and marginalized in their own city. And they decided they needed to be openhanded with the story God was writing at L&R Pallet.

It doesn't always work out this way, of course, but God blessed their obedience. Over the last year, *Forbes*, *Conscious Capitalism Magazine*, and TBN have all featured the remarkable story of redemption happening both in the lives of L&R Pallet staff and in the lives of the Ruders themselves. The more openhanded they've become, the more God's grace is on display.

The Ruders today understand love in a new way. Where they once found excitement and joy exclusively in what lay beyond their primary calling, today they find that excitement and joy loving the people within their reach. Where they once valued people for a purpose—getting to Peru—they have realized loving people *is* the purpose. Where they once desired to cling to *their precious*, today they offer all they have to those around them.

To fight the vice of lust, loving leaders:

1. **Develop a habit of love.** Although we are created to love, our hearts fall captive all too easily to rival gospels of lust and self-promotion. The heart is shaped by the "practices and rituals that you give yourself over to," notes author and speaker James K. A. Smith, a philosophy professor at Calvin College. Whether empowering employees to achieve their goals or celebrating the successes of a rival organization, love becomes habitual as we consistently seek out and act upon opportunities to serve one another. As we cultivate, refine, and develop our love, "it becomes a second nature that is humming along and guiding [us], and governing [us], and aiming [us] in certain directions without our realizing it."[17] Compassion International *institutionalizes* love by preserving 1 percent of their annual revenue to fund partner organizations in the countries where they work. In so doing, they commit themselves to blessing, encouraging, and strengthening their rivals, even when it does not benefit Compassion directly.

2. **Love people, use things (and never the opposite).** Gollum secured the mysterious, all-powerful Ring, but killed his

friend in the process. Ahab received the vineyard he lusted after at the cost of Naboth's life. In both instances, an unquenchable thirst for fulfillment led to a grave disregard for others. Take a step back and examine your mission. Do you trample people to accomplish it? Do you undermine a "rival" organization to reach your goals? Loving leaders prioritize people above any prize. As men and women made in the image of our Creator, our greatest expression of Christ isn't in what we do for Him, but in how we treat others along the way.

3. **Develop a community of accountability.** It's difficult to see when we are not acting in love. Invite others to help you see ways in which you are using people for your own purposes. To this end, one of the pioneers in the global sports ministry network regularly seeks out people who correct him. "I want people to tell me I'm wrong," he says. He gathered a community of people who would give him honest criticism. "We've built a culture of trust. These are people who are free to speak into each others' weaknesses, direction, purpose, and way of doing things."[18] As we are reminded in Hebrews 10:24–25, consider how you can "stir up one another to love and good works, not neglecting to meet together, as is the habit of some, but encouraging one another."

4. **Conduct listening sessions.** Actively and intentionally listen to employees to help identify ways to show care and concern for team members. At L&R Pallet, the process of rebuilding the company began by listening to the needs and challenges of their employees. These listening sessions shed light on the practical ways employees believed the company could improve. One outcome was adding

illustrations to all their training manuals. For employees who did not speak English as a first language, this created additional clarity and improved the overall safety of the company. Consider what love looks like within your organization, and then take advantage of opportunities to love others well.

REFLECTION QUESTIONS

1. What is your ultimate goal?
2. Have your goals become obsessions?
3. Who might be harmed in pursuit of your goals?
4. How has lust isolated you?
5. Both within and outside your organization, how can you better love your co-laborers?

CHAPTER 9

Envy vs. Contentment

	Scarcity	Abundance
Kingdom	II Misdirected (envy, vengeance)	IV Generous
Clan	I Excessive (greed, gluttony, lust)	III Deficient (sloth)

As Scott Harrison took center stage, I (Peter) was immediately struck by his red jeans, relaxed personality, and personal charisma.

"Who wears red jeans and actually pulls it off?" I wondered. Who was this guy?

Starting with his personal story, Scott shared how, as a former nightclub promoter, he took his knowledge of selling Bacardi drinks to found a nonprofit called charity: water that expanded access to clean water around the world. Listening to his tale of radical reversal with a truly innovative approach to raising funds for clean water, I was blown away. I did not remember ever hearing a more compelling story from a nonprofit leader.

Apparently I wasn't the only one impressed. Scott's charisma and innovative business model allowed charity: water to experience growth at a rate I'd never seen within the nonprofit realm. In just a few years, charity: water raised tens of millions of dollars for clean water.

Looking up at his red jeans, then down at my pleated khakis and button-down shirt—the uniform I'd worn since high school—I thought, "How in the world can I compete with Scott?"

Little did I know what a damaging thought that was going to be.

Shortly after my encounter with Scott came Kiva. For many months I couldn't start a conversation about HOPE International without someone interjecting, "Wait, have you heard of Kiva?"

Microfinance can be a hard sell, but when Jessica Jackley and Matt Flannery founded Kiva in 2005, they seemed to have found the silver bullet that broadened its appeal from the business community to the general population. By matching donors with a specific entrepreneur in need of funding, they successfully applied the compelling child-sponsorship model of fundraising to microfinance. Kiva exploded in popularity after being featured in the *New York Times* and on *Oprah*.

We had pitched HOPE to anyone who would listen, with limited success, but when Kiva came along, their growth seemed almost effortless. They had trouble keeping enough aspiring entrepreneurs on their website. Almost as soon as a profile was posted, the loan was fully funded. Kiva had a waiting list for would-be funders, while we had plenty of money left to raise to meet our core budget.[1]

The irony in being envious of Kiva's growth is that growth for Kiva was growth for microfinance. Kiva brought awareness of and excitement for microfinance where it had never existed before. We didn't have to work as hard to explain microfinance; Kiva had already done that. Even more, HOPE was actually a recipient of funds raised through Kiva, and we posted hundreds of entrepreneurs on their site. Yet to be honest, it was hard to see these benefits as I focused on what they had that I lacked.

To justify myself, I set to work reviewing other organizations' annual reports. In comparison to some nonprofits, I felt successful. We were, after all, growing quickly. But then I would look back to charity: water, Kiva, or so many others like them. Our growth rate, while strong, didn't compare to the growth rates of these standout nonprofits. I didn't have eyes to see anything other than *relative* growth. In my heart, I was dissatisfied. We were growing, but not like they were. God was moving, and people were responding, but *if only* I had Scott's stage presence, how much more could we accomplish? God had been good to us, but I wanted more.

> **ENVY:** craving for ourselves what God has given to others.

Richard Newhauser explains envy simply: "Sorrow over another's good fortune, joy at their misfortune."[2] It's very similar to the German word *schadenfreude*, joy in another's misery.

It's worse with those who are closest to you. Aristotle's definition of envy is close to Newhauser's, but with this added observation: envy is most acute among equals.[3] Most of us don't envy Bill Gates. He's completely out of our league. We envy the guy down the street with a sweeter ride than ours. We envy the peer who is now a step above us on the ladder despite entering our field at the same time we did. We envy the organizational leaders who seem to have it all together and are experiencing more rapid growth rates.

It shouldn't be surprising that many biblical examples of envy involve brothers. As we've already noted, Cain murders Abel after Abel's offering finds favor with God and his does not.[4] Joseph is sold into slavery by brothers envious of their father's deep love for a favored child.[5] The Prodigal Son's elder brother stands off at a distance, filled with bitterness while his father celebrates a son returned home.[6]

I don't want to be a destructive force against brothers and sisters in the Kingdom of God, and I don't even want envy to make me miss the party! When another leader or organization experiences a blessing, I want to be the first to celebrate.

My inability to rejoice with charity: water and Kiva revealed I had some work to do on my posture toward "rivals."

Relatively Successful

Any time we find our significance in a *relative* definition of success, we poison our hearts. Instead of evaluating our success by how faithful we are to the opportunities and abilities God has provided us, we slip into comparison.

It's a problem we believe affects many Christian ministries and Christ-followers and undermines our shared mission. We can identify this attitude in the goals we set:

We want to be the best in the industry.

We want to grow faster than our competition.

We want to bring in a greater share of donations to the sector.

They might sound noble, but these definitions of success are entirely relative. We are defining our success or failure based on a comparison to others.

Nothing crushes collaboration and friendship faster than comparison. Nothing good ever comes from it. There are two extremes: we either begin to believe that our organization is superior because our numbers look better, or we are crushed by comparison, becoming disheartened by the relative success of another organization.

Competition inhibits a giving spirit. Why would we want to share with others when we are measuring our success against theirs? It is a mindset that leads to insularity, trade secrets, and closed fists instead of open hands.

Envy = Kingdom Blight

Theodore Roosevelt famously said, "Comparison is the thief of joy." Evidence now confirms what has long been anecdotally true. Psychologist Jean Twenge writes of the deleterious effects of smartphone use on adolescents. While phones and social media were intended to connect us, they often isolate, as they highlight all that we are missing out on in comparison to others. Eighth-graders who heavily use social media increase their risk for depression by 27 percent.[7]

We believe envy is absolutely a contributing factor, and it's not only undermining adolescent friendships but also the Kingdom mentality to which we've been called. Pastor Robert Gelinas says it this way, "The whole time you're obsessing about the thing you can't have, you're missing out on the thing you're supposed to be obsessing about: 'Seek first the kingdom of God and his righteousness.'"[8]

God invites us to look outside ourselves not so we can compare, rank, and rate one another but because "Thy kingdom come, Thy will be done" is too lofty a goal to undertake alone.[9] When Paul wrote to the church in Corinth of the incredible—and incredibly diverse—spiritual gifts they had received, he wrote, "Are all apostles? Are all prophets? Are all teachers? Do all work miracles? Do all possess gifts of healing?"[10] Of course not, yet according to Paul, "to each is given the manifestation of the Spirit for the common good."[11] Acknowledging one another's gifts ought to help us see how we can best work together to advance our shared mission. But envy creeps in and corrupts, making us more aware of others in the Kingdom, yet simultaneously more isolated.

Henry Fairlie, a social commentator and essayist, commissioned Vint Lawrence to draw a picture of a person beset by each of the seven deadly sins to include in his book *The Seven Deadly Sins Today*. As Pastor Greg Lafferty of Willowdale Chapel shared, "After more than three decades in print, it's still one of the great works on the subject of the sins that have disrupted and destroyed humankind from the beginning of time."[12]

It is the artwork, as much as the text, that communicates with power and clarity.

Lawrence's illustration for envy is fittingly ugly. The person has his back pressed up to a door. On his side of the door, dark, nervous lines surround him. On the other side, white. There he sits in the dark, squinting his slanted, monstrous eyes so he can catch a glimpse of the light through a tiny keyhole. Beyond that door—we're left to imagine—there are people. Beautiful, wealthy, highly-skilled people. He is trapped by his envy, and all he can do is look out and yearn.

We don't actually see what's on the other side of the door. Nor do we see what's beyond the person on his side of the door. That's fitting because it doesn't matter. Envy is less about circumstances and more about the condition of our hearts. In our two-by-two, envy resides in the externally-focused, scarcity-perceiving quadrant. Envy requires an awareness of what lies beyond: our eyes peering through a keyhole into a room we don't inhabit. Yet when we are gripped by a scarcity mentality, we see the good in someone else's life not as cause for joy or celebration but rather as a direct assault on our own prospects. Because they seem full, we remain empty.

Tim Keller says that at its core, envy is a failure to trust God to fulfill us.[13] And looking for fulfillment in anything else—our work, our relationships, our bank account—will cause us to find fault with it. We have this huge, overwhelming desire to find what's missing in our lives. And this feeling is exacerbated when we see images and hear the experiences of others who seem to have grasped the happiness, joy, or success we pursue.

The most prominent part of Lawrence's illustration is a giant, teardrop-shaped abdomen. There's a huge void right in the center of this guy's belly. His stomach is bloated but empty—and he wants to fill it.

The last of the Ten Commandments is "You shall not covet." The antidote might be found in the first: "You shall have no other gods."[14] If you don't want to break the last, you need to practice the first.[15]

The Antidote to Envy

There are two common ways to respond to our inability to fill the void in our hearts. One is to say that since we know our best efforts to fill ourselves will be futile, why bother trying? If we simply give up on looking for things to put in that giant, teardrop-shaped abdomen, we will be like the one Qoheleth warns against in Ecclesiastes 4:5: "The fool folds his hands and eats his own flesh." When we don't labor to feed our body, it eats itself.

The other fallacy is to grasp at life with both hands, striving to acquire as much as possible to fill it with two-handed gusto. But that's not the way either. This is the wisdom Scripture repeats time and time again. Proverbs 15:16–17 says, "Better is a little with the fear of the Lord than great treasure and trouble with it. Better is a dinner of herbs where love is than a fattened ox and hatred with it." The options are tranquility, love, and fear of the Lord or striving, turmoil, and hatred. 1 Timothy 6:6 repeats, "Godliness with contentment is great gain." Proverbs 14:30 says, "A tranquil heart gives life to the flesh, but envy makes the bones rot."

We can fold our hands like the sluggardly fool and eat ourselves, or we could become like the striving fool who tries to grab everything he can with two hands until envy rots his bones. Both are self-defeating, self-destructive behaviors. Author Shauna Niequist says, "If you invest yourself deeply in what *is* [one handful], instead of distracting yourself with what is not, or what could be, or what might be happening somewhere else, your life will be infinitely richer. . . . There will always be more joy in your life if you're present to what is than if you live with your face pressed up against the glass of someone else's life."[16]

There is a third way, though it seems to be a path few tread. To find it, we may have to unfriend Facebook or say goodbye to Instagram, or, in my (Peter's) case, step away from other organizations' annual reports. But the journey to contentment is a worthwhile one, especially because it is found in trusting our gracious God, giver of "every good gift and every perfect gift."[17]

> **CONTENTMENT:** peace and fullness in God and what has been entrusted to us.

Psalm 16 is a powerful song of contentment. David writes, "I say to the LORD, 'You are my Lord; I have no good apart from you.' . . . The lines have fallen for me in pleasant places; indeed, I have a beautiful inheritance. . . . You make known to me the path of life; in your presence there is fullness of joy; at your right hand are pleasures forevermore."[18]

There may be seasons of life when these words come easily, but what about when our mission seems thwarted? What about when others appear to have it so much easier? What about when we're being faithful to God's calling but we feel like it's all falling apart? Can we join the apostle Paul in saying, "I have learned in whatever situation I am to be content"?[19]

No Matter the Circumstances

Heather and David Moreno have learned contentment in the midst of a ministry that didn't go according to their plan. From the time Heather and David were married, there was no doubt in their minds that God was calling them to serve as missionaries overseas. The two spent many years in training and preparation before a call came asking them to join a team that would mobilize the Church to combat sex trafficking in Bangkok, Thailand. Heather and David recall their immediate assurance that this was the path God had laid out for their family. With David's experience as a pastor, Heather's training as a social worker, and their passion for Southeast Asia, the opportunity seemed tailor-made.

With no intention of returning to the United States, they left their jobs, sold their cars, and gave away most of their belongings. From the moment of their arrival in Thailand, Heather says, "We felt right at home."[20]

They arrived on the scene not as saviors but as students. They met with other groups working in the city, spent time getting to know the local Thai churches, and prioritized corporate prayer and worship with their team and others serving across the city.

As they learned more about the deeply entrenched problem of sex trafficking in Bangkok, it quickly became clear they couldn't go it alone. "The giant is a huge giant, and sometimes you feel like you're David," David shared. "We're throwing stones at it, but, Lord, when is it going to fall?"

Even as they studied Thai and laid the groundwork for the ministry they hoped to begin, Heather and David realized their best chance of slaying this giant would be to come at it as a united front. They had a rooting for rivals approach and were committed to coordinating the efforts of the many disparate groups working to serve the victims of sex trafficking. They made certain that Thai Christians—a small yet divided minority representing less than 1 percent of Thailand's population— joined expatriate missionaries in their service.

About six months into their time in Thailand, the Morenos joined their team for a spiritual retreat. A facilitator led their group in answering questions about their short- and long-term goals and fears. Their greatest fear, Heather recalls, was that they would someday have to leave this ministry and these people who had captured their hearts. It seemed improbable, as the two were united in their passion. They would leave only if it were a matter of life and death for their children, they agreed.

The couple was elated to learn shortly thereafter that they were expecting their second child. But a few months later doctors discovered that, due to a rare genetic condition, their son would be born with no immune system and would require a bone marrow transplant just after birth.

Their team threw a combined baby shower and goodbye party as, with torn hearts, Heather and David followed the advice of doctors and returned home—to no jobs, no house, and a great deal of uncertainty. "It was like getting the rug pulled out from under us," Heather says. "It was really hard sometimes to not ask 'Why?'" Though they had so clearly been called to this burgeoning ministry in Thailand, they found themselves back in Maryland, where they spent the better part of a year in the hospital and then in mandatory isolation to protect their son from germs.

All the while, the Morenos and those who love them prayed for a successful transplant that would enable their son to live a healthy life and free their family to return to Thailand. Heather and David remained full of faith for their son's healing. They avoided placing roots back home in Maryland, keeping them-selves "light on [their] feet," ready to return to Thailand as soon as doctors gave the word.

Yet the word didn't come. Today their son is healthy and thriving, but ongoing complications with his care require the family to stay stateside.

In the years that have passed, the Morenos have seen many missionaries to Thailand come and go, while their desire to re-turn has never wavered or subsided. "Even though it is difficult, the posture of our hearts is to continue serving and believing in the goodness of God," explains David.

The Morenos could have chosen envy, but instead have discov-ered contentment. The result was a decision to serve right where they were, instead of waiting to be back in Thailand. The More-nos created Advance Worldwide, a nonprofit that empowers the global Church to meet needs within their own local communities.

Pastor and author Robert Gelinas says, "Envy wants us to hate our life. . . . Envy wants us to be angry with God—*I can't believe You gave me this life.* Contentment [allows us to say], *I can't <u>believe</u> You gave me this life!*"[21] Though their lives and ministry have not been without challenges, Heather and David find themselves in this second category. "God has been faithful in using every experience in this journey with Him to shape our lives, our calling, and this dream we now have been allowed to release. We are expectant and excited for what lies ahead!" the Morenos shared.[22]

Practicing Contentment

We no longer measure our success by someone else's annual report. We no longer view fellow nonprofit workers as rivals but rather as co-laborers. When we hear of the prosperity of charity: water, Jobs for Life, or World Relief, we want to be the first to stand and cheer loudly at what God is doing. We want to support their work and help advance their missions because we believe their work brings us closer to "Thy kingdom come, Thy will be done."[23] We want to energetically work to introduce funders to other organizations and ministries whose missions align with the giving priorities God has placed on their hearts.

To combat the vice of envy, contented leaders:

1. **Realize comparison is a losing game.** Defining our organization's success in comparison to that of fellow nonprofits keeps us from rooting for our rivals. I didn't cheer Scott Harrison on in his vital work when I believed his success magnified my (relative) failure. When we measure our success against that of other leaders, we fall prey to envy or pride. Attempts to gain a competitive advantage come at great Kingdom cost, even if they seem to yield temporary organizational success.

2. **Ask God for a change of heart, not circumstances.** Envy and contentment are conditions of our heart, not our

circumstances. Even as our personal or organizational circumstances improve, we will find cause to envy others until our hearts have been transformed and set free from our faulty belief in scarcity. Because we serve the God who created all and sustains all, there is enough: more for someone else does not mean less for us. Practice gratefully acknowledging the areas of abundance already present in your organization. Collectively create routines that regularly recognize and celebrate God's many gifts.

3. **Send staff.** Leading from a place of contentment means that when a valued staff member feels called to another organization or when their gifts and abilities would have a greater impact somewhere else, we celebrate their new assignment. When staff leave HOPE, whether it's for a position at another international nonprofit organization or in the private sector, we celebrate the decision. We want to send staff members off well, and make time for a party and our prayers. Even when it comes to staffing, we want to resist territorialism and instead view such transitions through the lens of Kingdom contribution.

4. **Thank, ask at a 7:1 ratio.** In one study of more than 1,000 donors, researchers found that 87 percent of those surveyed associated their worst nonprofit experiences with organizations that "pestered" them to give.[24] Nonprofits are notoriously good at asking and bad at thanking and educating. Fundraising appeals are necessary but should be done in the right balance of thanking and educating donors on the impact of their generosity. We believe nonprofit leaders should find ways to say thank you seven times before earning the right to ask again. In so doing, leaders model contentment and eschew envy.

REFLECTION QUESTIONS

1. How do you respond when another organization gets a major win? If your response is not celebration, what is holding you back from celebrating others' successes?
2. Have you ever felt envious of another organization or leader? How did you respond?
3. Are you willing to share mistakes with others or will you keep them to yourself? Do you really want others to succeed when it feels like you're stuck? Why or why not?

CHAPTER 10

Vengeance vs. Grace

	Scarcity	Abundance
Kingdom	II Misdirected (envy, vengeance)	IV Generous
Clan	I Excessive (greed, gluttony, lust)	III Deficient (sloth)

Their friendship is perhaps the most unlikely in all of Colorado.

Jim Daly is the president of Focus on the Family, the evangelical family ministry headquartered in Colorado Springs. Ted Trimpa is a prominent Democratic Party strategist widely known for his influence in the gay rights movement in the United States.

On the political and worldview spectrum, it might be impossible to find two Coloradans further apart. And yet, Trimpa and Daly count each other dear friends and provide a powerful example of how to work side by side, even when you don't see eye to eye.

"Ted is not my enemy. He's somebody that Christ died for, just like me," shared Daly in a public conversation with Ted Trimpa at the Q Conference on a warm spring day in Denver in 2016. "All I want to do in my relationship with Ted is express that love."[1]

Together, Daly and Trimpa and the organizations they represent worked to dramatically strengthen Colorado's laws against human trafficking. Finding common ground, the pair led their divergent coalitions to work together to toughen the penalties for human-trafficking offenders and establish a council to examine the issue in the state.[2]

Daly and Trimpa had no apparent reason to forge a friendship that extended beyond their joint efforts to combat human trafficking. Frankly, they had every reason to exhibit hostility toward one another. Their respective organizations had been locked in combat for decades. Focus on the Family regularly lambasted Trimpa's agenda. Trimpa and the advocacy organizations he led regularly ridiculed Focus on the Family's agenda.

Trimpa's and Daly's organizations had a long, sad history of exchanging barbs in local newspapers and over the radio airwaves. But facing an opportunity to fuel the vitriol, Trimpa and Daly decided on a different approach: friendship. What began with a simple email of greeting grew into a deep friendship. From the start, they treated one another with "great civility," focused on a mutual desire to bring solutions, and refused to vilify each other to appease their divergent bases.[3]

"I have to tell you, and I mean this very sincerely," interjected Trimpa near the end of their conversation, "I feel [the love of God] every time we meet. I really do."[4]

As Trimpa shared about their friendship, his hand rested comfortably on Daly's shoulder. He paused to reflect, and then described his recent hospital stay following open heart surgery. He recalled with real affection how Daly stood by him through that trying season. "Someone who I knew who was always praying for me, was always checking on me, whose presence I could feel," Trimpa remembered, "was Jim."

Their friendship, built over years, stands as a sharp counterpoint to what seems like the normal course of business in modern life, even among Christian nonprofits. In an age of deep tribalism—where so many of our conversations are consumed by the issues dividing us—practicing grace across such deep religious and political lines can seem impossible.

Anglican Priest Tish Harrison Warren writes, "Communities can have opposing ideologies, yet not silence one another, but instead learn to live as neighbors and, more radically, as friends."[5]

Todd Peterson, profiled in chapter 4 for his role in promoting Bible translation collaboration among various agencies, believes that three principles and Christ-like attributes—generosity, humility, and integrity—lead to friendship and ultimately guide greater partnership.[6] When both (or all) parties honor these principles above their own agenda, the relationship thrives.

Trimpa and Daly risked a lot by even meeting together. Both have allies who say their friendship evidences compromise in their core beliefs. Others call their friendship a betrayal of the righteous anger they *should* exhibit on important issues. But taking up arms against those we consider rivals inhibits, not advances, our mission of proclaiming and demonstrating the love of Christ to the world around us.

Sitting in his office and reflecting on the positive outcomes of this unlikely friendship, Daly pondered, "I wonder what would happen if Christians prayed for the fruit of the Spirit to be exhibited in each and every conversation, and in each and every relationship."[7]

Baby Killers Work Here

Christians affirm the sanctity and dignity of all human life, particularly the most vulnerable human life. Abortion is a rallying issue because of just how defenseless the unborn are. They are voiceless, fragile human beings who are regularly victimized because a fetus holds no legal status, even after becoming viable outside the womb.

Our country's abortion laws stand in sharp contrast to most of the world. The United States is one of just seven countries— among the most permissive in the world—that allows for elective abortions after twenty weeks.[8] Since 1973, over fifty-nine million unborn babies have been aborted in the United States alone, according to statistics from the Centers for Disease Control and Guttmacher Institute.[9]

The number of abortions in the United States is thankfully falling, but still averaging about one million annually in recent years.[10] These staggeringly high numbers still drive many Christians and other pro-life activists to extreme measures. For them, when comparing the effects of abortion to other issues in our country, the protection of nearly one million American lives eclipses all other issues of life.

Just a few blocks from my (Chris's) home is a sprawling Planned Parenthood compound. I use that word quite literally. A ten-foot-tall fence surrounds the massive complex. Trees and hedges line the fence to block visibility from the street. And I understand why.

At least once a week, I see protesters lining up around the compound. They caravan into the neighborhood, stacking up ladders along the fences. Perched atop their ladders and looking down on the vulnerable women en route to their appointments, they hold signs with warnings and graphic images for the staff and expectant mothers to see.

I recently walked among the protesters, and I looked more closely at the signs. Scrawled on a poster board like one a spectator might hold up at a sporting event were the words, "Baby killers work here."

Ideologically, I share much in common with these protesters. I am dismayed by how our permissive laws create such little protection for these unborn babies, created in the very image of God. If we are serious about the demands of our faith, abortion is one of many causes toward which Christians should exhibit righteous anger. If something angers God, it should likewise anger us.

In Ephesians 4:26, Paul says, "Be angry and do not sin," acknowledging anger as a legitimate emotion for Christians. Passivity is not what Christ asked of His followers. "Anger is always an outgrowth of love," explains Pastor Tim Keller. "Anger is that which rouses you and rallies all of our faculties to defend that which you ultimately love. You get angry to the degree you love something."[11] If our loves are rightly ordered, there are times when we should and will be angry.

It is vengeance (or wrath), not anger, that is a deadly sin. We may use all these words interchangeably, but their connotation both in the Bible and throughout church history illuminates their differences. Anger is directed at injustice. Vengeance, though, distorts anger.

> **VENGEANCE:** ungoverned anger marked by bitterness, fits of rage, and rivalries with the world around us.

Vengeance is a form of misdirected love. Vengeful leaders believe God is not big enough to enact final justice. They believe vengeance is *theirs*, not God's. And it's this scarcity mindset about God's power that misdirects their love beyond their organizational borders. They see the world beyond their own, but their vision is clouded by the vengeance festering within their hearts.

"Beloved, never avenge yourselves," writes the apostle Paul to the Church in Rome, "but leave it to the wrath of God, for it is written, 'Vengeance is mine, I will repay, says the Lord.'"[12] While vengeance may accomplish our short-term goals, Scripture tells us vengeance "does not produce the righteousness of God."[13]

I don't know the hearts of the Planned Parenthood protesters who show up holding signs saying, "Baby killers work here." But what I've observed in their behavior seems more in keeping with a host of actions described in Galatians 5 as "against the Spirit" ("enmity, strife, jealousy, fits of anger, rivalries, dissensions, divisions") than the fruits of the Spirit outlined just a few verses later ("love, joy, peace, patience, kindness, goodness, faithfulness, gentleness, and self-control").[14]

I haven't just seen this in passionate protestors; I've seen it in a more discreet yet equally destructive and disruptive form among nonprofit leaders.

Cassian, Evagrius, and others who did some of the earliest work on the Seven Deadly Sins said anger *toward other people* almost always disrupts our relationship with others and with God. As Rebecca Konyndyk DeYoung summarizes, "Most of the time, most of your anger is destructive."[15]

From our vantage point, it sure appears these protesters' response to Planned Parenthood staff members and expectant mothers—men and women who, like unborn babies, are created in God's image—falls short of kind, gentle, peaceful, and patient. When we contrast their approach with the approach of Joe Baker and Save the Storks, we see an alternative way to influence and impact others that addresses the injustice toward unborn babies without compromising the values we hold as followers of Christ.

Donuts > Poster Boards

"When we decide to park our sonogram buses in front of abortion clinics," said Joe Baker, founder of Save the Storks, "instead of going there and yelling and calling abortion clinic employees names, we made it our mission to really learn *their* names, and get to know them, and reach out to them."[16]

Baker founded Save the Storks to respond creatively to one of the most contentious issues in our country. Their primary means of accomplishing their mission is through equipping local pregnancy resource centers with sonogram buses. These buses, staffed by trained ultrasound technicians, park in neighborhoods with high rates of unplanned pregnancies.

The strategy Baker and his team use is one rooted in love and friendship. Rather than name-calling and scare tactics, employees in Save the Storks buses employ the counterintuitive strategy modeled by Jesus: They love and serve. They choose grace.

It's not uncommon for these employees to take donuts to abortion clinic staff as a simple act of love.

In Florida, an abortion doctor named Ali Azimi approached the Save the Storks bus recently and said, "We obviously disagree about the issue of abortion. However, some of my patients change their minds about going through with the abortion, and I've never had someone I could refer them out to. And I refer them out to you guys."

"We were floored by what a little kindness could do," reflected Baker.

> **GRACE:** serving our neighbors, even those we might deem undeserving, with outrageously generous love and tenderness.

Ginny Payne saw firsthand how grace overcomes vengeance.[17] As a director of Fresno/Madera Youth for Christ's (YFC) Parent Life ministry in Fresno, she regularly served teen girls with unplanned pregnancies through relational Christian ministry. Coincidentally, the Youth for Christ office is close to the Planned Parenthood campus. A few years ago, after Payne became acquainted with the director of the Fresno Planned Parenthood, he invited her to come and share about Youth for Christ with his staff.

"They're only two blocks from here," Payne said. "They're getting picketed every single day out in front of where they work. Every single day. That's their impression of Christians."

Much like the picketers, Payne strongly disagrees with the way the Planned Parenthood staff express their concern for women. But rather than come into that meeting with her spikes up, she came in a posture of grace for the scorn these workers had experienced so regularly each day of their working lives. When she walked into Planned Parenthood's office, she did so with a great deal of angst as she wrestled to find the balance between truth and love.

"I had to go through five different locked doors to get to that boardroom. Five locked doors. What are they locking in or locking out? Before I spoke, I realized: they're just as afraid of me as I'm afraid of them. I was able to speak with empathy because I was there as someone who loved the girls they work with."

Because of the ongoing grace exhibited and trust established by Payne and her colleagues, Fresno/Madera Youth for Christ earned a number of referrals from Planned Parenthood. Because they led with love, doors opened for them to invest relationally in vulnerable girls, sharing the hope and grace of Christ with them in their time of pain.

Leading with Grace

One of the girls Planned Parenthood referred to YFC we'll call "Lindsey." Payne and her team welcomed Lindsey with open arms. "She had had an abortion and expected us to not value her," Payne said. Payne was grateful for the opportunity to prove otherwise.

Through a relationship with a Youth for Christ mentor—who had herself had an abortion earlier in life—Lindsey began to slowly rebuild her life. Both Lindsey and the staff at this Planned Parenthood had clear assumptions about followers of Christ. They had known only vengeance. Rightly or wrongly, they associated followers of Christ with rage, bitterness, and scorn.

Nobody who knows Jim Daly, Joe Baker, or Ginny Payne would say they lack righteous anger about the issues central to the heart of God. Their love is not a blind, unthinking, justice-free love. But everyone who knows them would say their love is marked by grace.

For leaders of faith-based organizations, exhibiting grace toward political opponents and adversaries of all sorts can feel both unattainable and risky. Like Daly's and Trimpa's friends, Christian leaders can view these sorts of friendships as a potential betrayal of convictions. When news surfaced that Daly and Focus on the Family were partnering with Ted Trimpa to pass House Bill 1273, many donors—including some who gave significantly—cut off funding to Focus on the Family as a means of expressing their displeasure.

"Some donors called and said, 'Listen, if you work with people like him, I'm not going to support you anymore,'" Daly said. "For me, that's not acceptable." Daly told these donors they can keep their cash.

Daly and Trimpa found and pursued common ground and, ultimately, furthered God's Kingdom by combatting one of the most grievous injustices of our day. To do so required them to forsake vengeance and embrace grace. They were openhanded with their friendship, allowing God to do the work He intended in and through their relationship.

As leaders of faith-based organizations, we are commanded to follow the example of Jesus and "love our enemies," and seek friendships with our ideological opposites. On the ideological spectrum, many of Jesus' closest friends were separated by as wide a chasm as Daly and Trimpa.[18] Yet these relationships were built upon the foundation of understanding "how important it is sometimes to disagree—but not to separate,"[19] wrote Fred Smith, president of The Gathering.

Real friendship exists on a currency of trust. As friendships deepen, trust multiplies, allowing friends to seek opportunities for collaboration while remaining steadfast in convictions. "Love even for enemies is the key to the solution of the problems of our world," Rev. Martin Luther King Jr. once wrote in a sermon. "Love is the only force capable of transforming an enemy into a friend."[20]

King wrote these words not from his office but from a jail cell, imprisoned by men who viewed his freedom as a danger to society. In that same sermon, King cited the way American hero Abraham Lincoln pursued grace over revenge and friendship over rivalry.

Team of Rivals

Abraham Lincoln possessed a knack for making friends.

In her biography on Lincoln, *Team of Rivals*, historian Doris Kearns Goodwin described Lincoln as a man who won the Republican nomination in part because of his "unusually loyal circle of friends."[21] And as Goodwin notes, "No political circle was more loyally bound than the band of compatriots working for Lincoln."[22]

Heading into the Republican primary in the spring of 1860, few expected Lincoln to win his party's nomination. Running against former governors and more well-known politicians, Lincoln's victory surprised the nation. It even surprised Lincoln, who had no expectation of victory.

After winning the primary and then the general election, Lincoln upended political norms by elevating his former rivals rather than banishing them. As soon as Lincoln occupied the White House, his ability to create trust and friendship—even with those some described as his enemies—was instantly on display.

"Do I not destroy my enemies when I make them my friends?" Lincoln famously asked.[23]

Lincoln could have exclusively elevated loyal allies who had helped him secure the nomination. He could have limited his circle of friends to those who had already proven their allegiance to him and to his leadership. And he could have punished his opponents, choosing vengeance and inflicting revenge. Instead, Lincoln opted for a rare political strategy: grace.

During his presidency, he appointed all three of his Republican primary opponents to his cabinet, believing these men were capable leaders best suited for the posts, regardless of the toxic way they had spoken about Lincoln on the campaign trail. He also appointed several Democrats to his cabinet, including Edwin Stanton to the important post of secretary of war.

This was particularly surprising because Stanton, a big-city lawyer, had earlier snubbed Lincoln, who practiced law in the small town of Springfield, Illinois. It's reported Stanton labeled Lincoln a "backwoods bumpkin" and discarded Lincoln's counsel on a case Lincoln had invested considerable hours in preparing.

"Lincoln had an internal confidence," Goodwin reflected. "He was able to put those past rivalries beside him knowing that if these guys do a good job, then it will only be down to the interest of the country."[24]

Though his former rivals surely viewed their cabinet appointments suspiciously, Lincoln quickly won them over. Reporter Horace White noted Lincoln embodied "keen intelligence, genuine kindness of heart, and the promise of true friendship."[25]

During his presidency, Lincoln demonstrated grace and affection for the diverse group of leaders assembled around him. He consistently assumed positive intent from his cabinet members, even when Lincoln had the right to be suspicious. He was first to apologize when conflicts arose. And, in a strategy as apt today as it was then, he famously wrote his most honest frustrations in "hot letters" to these leaders that were "never sent, never signed."[26]

His grace for political rivals in no way meant Lincoln lacked clarity in his convictions. He would regularly communicate his positions to his cabinet, knowing some would disagree with him. He would clearly state he was settled in his position, but he would still open up the floor for feedback so his advisors could voice their dissent.

With his upside-down approach to leadership, Abraham Lincoln became one of the most important leaders in American history. With a team of rivals, Lincoln held together a coalition that abolished slavery and ended the Civil War.

After Lincoln's assassination, the country was crushed, including many who initially held Lincoln in real contempt. Edwin Stanton's private secretary wrote Stanton after Lincoln's death, saying, "Not everyone knows, as I do, how close you stood to our lost leader, how he loved you and trusted you, and how vain were all the efforts to shake that trust and confidence."[27]

Abraham Lincoln's legacy stands on two pillars of his leadership philosophy. First, he treated his former rivals not as political pawns but as trusted advisors and beloved friends. And second, he appointed rivals based on their shared interest in abolishing slavery. This prevailing common interest allowed Lincoln to work together even with leaders he strongly disagreed with on other important matters.

Bad Company

Does grace toward our ideological opposite mean we always partner, always accommodate, always compromise?

Appointing our ideological opposites to leadership positions within our faith-based organizations isn't usually a wise strategy, for reasons we've outlined extensively in *Mission Drift*.[28] And practicing grace and building friendships with those we might consider opponents—as modeled by Jim Daly, Joe Baker, and Ginny Payne—does not mean Christians ought always to be accommodating.

It is true the pages of Scripture are full of stories of people practicing grace. Knowing He would be betrayed, Jesus still humbled himself and washed Judas's feet.[29] Even though they were political enemies, the Good Samaritan served the Jewish man wounded and abandoned on the roadside.[30] Hosea received back Gomer, despite her consistent infidelities.[31]

At the same time, it is also true God's people are instructed to be "wise as serpents and innocent as doves."[32] One can practice both grace and shrewdness.

We can extend grace to those with whom we hold deep disagreements without wavering in our own commitments. "We retain confidence in our beliefs, even when we recognize that they often stem from premises that others don't share," wrote John Inazu, law professor at Washington University.[33]

Partnering on shared interests does not mean we share the same beliefs. It is important for our witness and integrity as Christians that we make this clear. In the case of the people of Israel, it was this confusion that so often caused pain and heartache.

God commissioned Abraham, saying that through his descendants "shall all the nations of the earth be blessed."[34] God established His people as a refuge and beacon for not just the descendants of Abraham but for all the families of the earth. But time and again, God's people confused this command. God's people were to receive refugees and immigrants with generosity. But they were not commanded to adopt and anoint the practices of neighboring kingdoms as their own.

"There is a point at which strategy becomes its own form of idolatry—an attempt to manipulate the levers of history in favor of the causes we support," wrote Andy Crouch for

Christianity Today.[35] "Strategy becomes idolatry, for ancient Israel and for us today, when we make alliances with those who seem to offer strength."

The apostle Paul put it even more plainly when he said, "Do not be deceived: 'Bad company ruins good morals.'"[36]

When we lose sight of *who we are*, we sacrifice our identity for our strategy.

In the epic tale *Prince Caspian*, C. S. Lewis describes a moment when the Narnians find themselves close to defeat. Up against a powerful foe, Prince Caspian has assembled a ragtag army not formidable enough to resist the powerful Telmarines. The pragmatic dwarf warrior Nikabrik suggests Narnia consider a powerful ally.

"We want power: and we want a power that will be on our side," Nikabrik compellingly argues to his comrades. "Shall we go farther up for you, up to the crags? There's an Ogre or two and a Hag that we could introduce you to, up there."[37]

The hag Nikabrik references is the infamous White Witch, the sorceress long banished from Narnia. Some among Caspian's fledgling army are shocked by Nikabrik's suggestion.

Trufflehunter, a sage member of the resistance warns Nikabrik, "We should not have Aslan for friend if we brought in *that* rabble."[38]

But Nikabrik persists with making his case. "I'll believe in anyone or anything," said Nikabrik, "that'll batter these cursed barbarians to pieces or drive them out of Narnia. Anyone or anything, Aslan *or* the White Witch."[39]

The allure of power and influence is not a new temptation for followers of Jesus. Since the beginning of time, we have been offered power in exchange for our reliance upon God and truth. It's a seductive invitation, but extending grace does not mean we abandon the truth we hold most dearly.

Reimagining Friendship

Abe Lincoln invited his rivals to serve on his cabinet, but he did not bend on outlawing slavery. Jim Daly befriended and worked together with Ted Trimpa, but he did not endorse every policy for which Trimpa advocated. Ginny Payne and Joe Baker loved and served the staff and clients of abortion clinics, but they did not waver in their fight against abortion.

What Nikabrik missed was this: grace never forces us to forsake our most cherished beliefs. What Jim Daly, Martin Luther King Jr., Abraham Lincoln, and Trufflehunter understood was that true grace and real friendship do not demand we become a sanitized version of ourselves. King didn't agree with the men who jailed him. Abraham Lincoln didn't agree with Edwin Stanton's assessment of his intelligence. Ginny Payne doesn't agree with Planned Parenthood's definition of personhood. These sorts of friendships can feel impossible for people of deep conviction. Yet they are not only possible but essential if we are to bridge the growing divides in our world.

Evan Low is a Democratic California Assembly member who chairs the California Legislative Lesbian, Gay, Bisexual, and Transgender Caucus, and Barry Corey is the president of Biola University, an evangelical college in Los Angeles. They've become friends and stated, "You don't need to see eye to eye to work shoulder to shoulder."[40]

Gracious leaders still display righteous anger. They are confident in their beliefs and unafraid of befriending those who do not share them. They are openhanded in their friendships, knowing loving relationships can exist even when there is not alignment on all issues. And they model humility, acknowledging their own stereotypes and faults first, before pointing them out in others.

The friendships featured in this chapter stand as a sharp rebuke to Christian leaders. They are examples of people finding common ground across seemingly impossible divides. If these types of partnerships and friendships are possible, how much easier should it be for brothers and sisters in Christ to partner together? How much easier for us to discover common ground and areas for partnership with people we will spend all eternity alongside? If these men and women with radically different beliefs can effectively work together, how is it that Christian faith-based organizations still struggle to work beyond our boundaries?

Just as Lincoln realized extending grace to his rivals would advance the "interest of the country," perhaps it's time for us to extend grace to advance the interest of the Kingdom. And in so doing, may we learn to act like the family we are.

Practicing Grace

To fight the vice of vengeance, gracious leaders:

1. **Take risks.** Ted Trimpa and Jim Daly's deep friendship did not materialize out of the mist. Jim Daly extended a figurative olive branch to Ted Trimpa, inviting him to meet for an initial conversation. What transpired wasn't something either of them had planned, but it was an encouragement to them both—even if unlikely. They were openhanded with what might happen, but Daly took a risk by initiating.

   When Kathryn Joyce penned *The Child Catchers*,[41] a scathing book about Christians abusing the international adoption system, and a related op-ed in the *New York Times*,[42] it put many evangelicals on the defense. With merit, many believed Joyce's perspective painted an unfair picture of Christians. It's this context that made

Jedd Medefind's risk even more heartening. Medefind, president of the Christian Alliance for Orphans (CAFO), invited Joyce to a public discussion at the CAFO annual summit. "To listen well and seek to learn from those with whom we disagree helps us see our own blind spots and reflects the character of Jesus," the session overview summarized.[43]

Knowing both when and with whom to take these risks is more art than science. But leaders understand the importance of establishing and nurturing authentic friendships, even with those with whom they disagree strongly.

2. **Elevate the dialogue.** Ginny Payne did not settle for small talk with the local director of Planned Parenthood. She saw that initial meeting not as a simple meet-and-greet but as an opportunity to learn more about her counterpart's motivations, hopes, and dreams, both for his life and for his organization. Their partnership germinated out of that process of mutual discovery. Leaders like Payne see every moment as an opportunity to learn, grow, and connect.

3. **Write hot letters.** Abe Lincoln regularly wrote out his deepest, most visceral grievances in letters toward his rivals—and never sent them. In a digital age, this practice could not be more relevant. Rather than responding in anger when we've been wronged, perhaps instead write that angry email or letter to yourself or to God, voicing your most honest frustrations. When we read the Psalms, it's clear David practiced this regularly. Goodness, our Bible has a whole book titled *Lamentations*. Practicing grace doesn't mean we ignore when we've been wronged but rather that we govern our anger and eschew vengeance.

4. **Refuse to compromise on the essentials.** Over the last few years, there have been several large corporations that have placed strings upon their funding that would have forced HOPE to deny the beliefs we hold most dearly. Specifically, they said their funding was contingent upon HOPE hiring people without regard for their religious convictions. Refusing these substantial donations was not easy, but partnering with these companies would have required us to lie about our uniquely Christian identity. We hire Christians exclusively, which prevented us from continuing our partnership with these companies. We honored the relationship in the process, though, thanking them for their past support and wishing them well in their future endeavors. Likewise, they noted their appreciation for HOPE, and a friendship continued, even though the partnership did not.

5. **Seek to serve.** When Lincoln invested in friendships with his former rivals, it surely felt like a waste of his time. He had important work to do—abolishing slavery, ending the Civil War, holding the country together—but he chose perhaps the least expedient way to lead the country. It required that he take risks with his cabinet selection. It demanded he bury his own ego and find ways to dignify and help men who had done little to deserve his help.

REFLECTION QUESTIONS

1. When have you crossed the line from righteous anger to sinful anger or vengeance?
2. Have you placed a higher priority on your work or on building friendships? How can the two go hand in hand?

3. Do you consider it a threat or an opportunity when people or organizations oppose your own beliefs?

4. What are some of the passions and goals you have in common with those you have considered "rivals"?

5. Have any of your friendships caused you to seriously compromise your personal beliefs?

CHAPTER 11

Sloth vs. Steadfastness

	Scarcity	Abundance
Kingdom	II Misdirected (envy, vengeance)	IV Generous
Clan	I Excessive (greed, gluttony, lust)	III Deficient (sloth)

(Chris) glanced down at my phone and my stomach dropped. There, I saw the opening lines of a new message from Josh Heaston.

"Chris," he wrote, "You do not know me, but I am a pastor on staff with the YMCA of Greater Indianapolis and am helping to lead a rebirth of the YMCA Christian mission locally, nationally, and globally."[1]

The reason for my angst was the pretext. I knew what this message would be about. We had just published *Mission Drift*. In it, one of the longest, harshest case studies we featured was the complicated history of the Young Men's Christian Association (YMCA).

George Williams founded the YMCA to serve youth living in the London slums in the early 1800s. He launched the YMCA by leading Bible studies and prayer meetings for these young men. And, as its name indicated, Jesus was at the organization's core. The YMCA grew, fueled by Williams's vision.

"Let it never be forgotten that the foundations of the Young Men's Christian Association were laid in a prayer meeting in an upper room, in the fervent, effectual prayers of two young men," wrote J. E. Hodder Williams.[2]

But, over time, many YMCA leaders in the United States began to emphasize its fitness programs and downplay its uniquely Christian identity. Outside the United States, though, the YMCA has retained a more vibrant Christian distinctiveness. I've witnessed this firsthand when I've visited YMCAs in both Hong Kong and Singapore. There, you'd never miss why George Williams founded the organization. This is not always the case in much of the United States.

When the message arrived, I assumed Heaston wrote to protest our version of the YMCA's history. We were cautious in how we shared case studies in *Mission Drift*—as we've attempted to be in *Rooting for Rivals*—anonymizing sensitive stories and only naming names when the information was readily available publicly. But because of the clear public record, we didn't mince words about the Y's story of drift.

To my relief and surprise, Heaston wrote not a message of protest, but a gracious message acknowledging we had gotten the story *mostly* right. But his message didn't stop there. He went on to share an unwritten story of resurgence unfolding at the YMCA nationwide.

"God is once again doing something mighty through the YMCA," he said.

Heaston asked if I'd be open to hearing *that* story. What he shared in a follow-up phone call challenged assumptions I had about the YMCA and, more broadly, reminded me that because of the power of the Gospel, no person, nor any organization, should ever be written off. No matter how difficult their path, Heaston held on to hope. I hung up the phone grateful for Heaston's courage, excited about the work he pursued, and overwhelmed by the power of God.

Heaston understood the importance of the YMCA's mission and was working diligently on a complicated and difficult internal turnaround. Not an easy assignment, but one he believed in so much that he was willing to invest his life in it.

Abandoning Hope

Sloth is the final vice included in our two-by-two. It appears in quadrant III, where we understand God's abundance but remain focused on our clan. "Sloth is not to be confused with laziness," explains author and theologian Frederick Buechner. "A slothful man . . . may be a very busy man. He is a man who goes through the motions, who flies on automatic pilot."[3]

Or, as Rebecca Konyndyk DeYoung said, "Sloth is a laziness to love."[4]

It was Gregory the Great, in the sixth century, who first condensed the eight deadly sins into seven. The list of eight categorized by Evagrius a few hundred years earlier included *despair* and *apathy* (also labeled *sadness* and *sloth*, as in chapter 4) as distinct sins.[5] Gregory combined the two into one, and it's this combination that Buechner aptly describes. Sloth is a despairing apathy. If lust exists when we exhibit untamed desire, sloth exists when we exhibit no desire at all.

Sloth conjures images of the animal bearing its name and of that friend who considers napping a spiritual gift. But as Buechner notes, laziness is a byproduct of sloth, not its core. The danger of sloth is far deeper, and its effects on leaders far more pervasive, than we might think—even for the busiest of leaders.

> **SLOTH:** a deep-set, despairing apathy about the world within and beyond our organizational boundaries.

Proverbs tells us, "The soul of the sluggard craves and gets nothing."[6]

This lethargic posture typifies slothfulness. Slothful leaders might yearn for things of meaning, but they've lost the will to fight for them. Many have illuminated the real meaning of sloth by pointing to marriage.[7] Even if a spouse is working eighty hours a week or engaged in incredible service at home or in church, that spouse is in danger of slothfulness if he or she loses the will to fight for his or her marriage. Marriage requires the daily fight against the "laziness to love."

At the risk of over-generalizing, we'll say this: lazy people don't often pursue roles in nonprofit leadership. There are far less demanding ways to earn a living. Yes, laziness is a symptom of sloth, but it's likely not a symptom suffered by readers of this book. More commonly among faith-based nonprofit leaders, sloth manifests in the companion ills of busyness and cynicism.

Sloth should be unthinkable for Christian leaders. The central message of the Scriptures is one of enduring hope. The story of God and people is a story of a relentless Rescuer who secured our redemption and invited us to be part of His work of restoration. It is the story of God never giving up on us and inviting us to never give up on those around us.

But spend enough time with nonprofit leaders, and it's easy to see how we could succumb to sloth. We can attest just how maddening nonprofit work can be. Fundraising can be a bear. We serve in challenging communities and help deeply hurting people. Our boards and staffs can be wrought with conflicting visions and egos. Partnering with other organizations can be slow and frustrating. And we often face scrutiny and interference from critics, regulators, and government officials. Nonprofit work can feel defeating.

Seemingly insurmountable challenges can drive us toward busyness. We lose ourselves in bureaucracy, filling our schedules and imaginations with issues and work far downstream from the heart of our mission. If we're honest, we revel in our busyness. But in our hearts, we've lost our first love.

Or, these challenges drive us toward cynicism. Even if we put on a happy face with the public and with our donors, our hopes fade and darken. Beaten down by the challenges around us, we resign ourselves to pessimism and bitterness.

If anyone should have felt this way, it would have been Josh Heaston. He and his allies at the YMCA faced stiff odds and strong headwinds. That's what made what he shared so remarkable.

Holding on to Hope

When Heaston and I met—first over the phone and then in person—what immediately struck me was his hopefulness. He was aware of all the challenges facing the YMCA. He knew better than I what he was up against. But though there were ample reasons for discouragement, Heaston held on to hope. He wasn't expecting an easy or quick turnaround. But that did not defeat or dissuade him.

"You are right; we have drifted significantly," Heaston told me when we met.

He went on to share some of the behind-the-scenes challenges he and his cadre of YMCA leaders from across the country were facing. In short, the situation is complicated. Each YMCA chapter in the United States is a unique entity with its own board of directors. It's true, he said, that many YMCAs nationally have become little more than fitness centers. But in many key chapters around the country, local YMCAs have held fast to the founding mission. And they've begun spreading this message loud and wide.

"We're here to love, serve, and care for people in the same way Christ did," Heaston said. "There is something internally in every person on the planet that they want to be served, loved, and cared for. And the Y wants to be there to impact people in those ways. This vision has caught fire, and it's all about Christ. We are here to love, serve, and care for people in the same way Christ would."

Today, this group—the US Mission Network—gathers leaders from across the Y to pray, share best practices, and encourage one another to persevere. Their goal is to unite "in an effort to preserve, nurture and advance the Christian heritage and purpose of the YMCA across America."[8]

With funding from a few of the largest chapters and a few key foundations, this group has even hired a few staff members specifically charged with retelling the founding story and mission of George Williams and the YMCA to board members and executive directors across the country.[9]

More than anything, Heaston and his allies are peddling hope. And they're doing so with the prayer support and advocacy of YMCA leaders from across the world who are standing with this resurgent group of American YMCA leaders.

"We are visiting YMCA leadership teams in small towns, big cities, and everything in between," Heaston said. "We want to be more intentional about the Christian witness of the YMCA."[10]

They meet some leaders who are resistant to hearing that story. Others are disinterested. But some, Heaston shares, are surprised and energized by what they hear. They're encouraged to know there are other YMCA chapters leading the way in practicing a full-bodied approach to ministry in their communities. Some leave these conversations with a renewed commitment to recapturing the full, holistic mission of the YMCA.

"Sloth puts our souls to sleep," writer and pastor Robert Gelinas said. "Hope wakes them up."[11]

The US Mission Network faces long odds of changing everyone's opinions about the YMCA. But the entire effort, like Heaston himself, is characterized by its steadfastness in hope.

> **STEADFASTNESS:** a posture of enduring hope and ongoing commitment, even against seemingly insurmountable external and internal challenges.

"The future is bright," Heaston said. "I'm looking forward to giving the rest of my life to these efforts."

Steadfast leaders like Josh Heaston exhibit confidence in the goodness of God and in knowing how this grand story ends. They model the hope offered by their relentless Rescuer. They exhibit "strength for today and bright hope for tomorrow," as poet Thomas Chisholm wrote in "Great Is Thy Faithfulness."

Reasons for optimism within the YMCA are growing. Because of God's faithfulness and Heaston's and the US Mission Network's steadfastness, like-minded pastors are planting churches in YMCAs (close to fifty such churches exist across the country already, seven of which were planted in 2017 alone).[12] Their recognition of their need for churches and other Christian ministries has been vital in reclaiming their original mission. Steadfastness in fulfilling their mission has meant they've needed to ally themselves with other organizations committed to the same objectives, such as these churches, and parachurch ministries like Youth for Christ.

Still, Heaston does not know if he'll see the change he hopes for in his lifetime. He is not ignorant of the personal and institutional challenges he faces in accomplishing these goals. But the US Mission Network has not pinned their identity or hopes to their objectives, freeing them to celebrate the ways God provides along the way.

A slothful leader, characterized by a clan-focused abundance mentality, would look at the YMCA and say things are good enough. The Y serves a valuable purpose, even in communities where it focuses solely on fitness. A slothful leader would say, "Why seek more?" in the face of resistance or even opposition. But Heaston remains steadfast, and he won't allow the enormity of his task to dampen his hope. For he anchors his confidence in a *bright hope*, a hope unfazed by current circumstances and captivated by the Rescuer who will one day make all things new.

Too Busy to Care

Sloth is "a resistance to love's demands," writes Rebecca Konyndyk DeYoung.[13]

British essayist Dorothy Sayers writes sloth "is the sin which believes in nothing, cares for nothing, seeks to know nothing, interferes with nothing, enjoys nothing, loves nothing, hates nothing, finds purpose in nothing, lives for nothing, and only remains alive because there is nothing it would die for."[14]

If anyone could be immune to slothful leadership, it ought to be faith-based nonprofit leaders. Our work is defined by our care and concern for the missions entrusted to us. We joined our schools, pregnancy counseling centers, and missions agencies because of the depth of our concern. We should relish the hard work of partnering with other organizations and celebrating the successes of our peer organizations.

But if we're honest, many of us wake up each day consumed not by the missions etched in plaques and extolled in annual reports—nor with the larger mission we're in pursuit of together—but by the monotonous, unglamorous, and sometimes maddening realities of nonprofit life. If we aren't distracted by the mundane or jaded by past challenges, we may simply be overwhelmed by the amount of good work there is to do. Some days, changing the world looks like emptying a never-ending inbox or hopping on another plane away from loved ones at home.

The story Jesus tells us about the Good Samaritan is a rallying parable: one that affirms the importance of the work we do as faith-based organizations of all varieties. In this story, we are eager to identify with the charitable Samaritan. "But a Samaritan, as he journeyed, came to where [the wounded man] was, and when he saw him, he had compassion. He went to him and bound up his wounds, pouring on oil and wine. Then he set him on his own animal and brought him to an inn and took care of him."[15]

Ah, there we are, we think. Whether it's helping a family hoping to adopt a child, counseling a student struggling in our residence hall, or writing an essay decrying one of our society's ills, we look at the Good Samaritan as if we're looking in a mirror.

But what if our mirror showed not the Samaritan, but the Levite or the priest? Honest leaders will admit that often we have far more in common with these religious leaders than the hero of the story. Occupationally, the Levite and priest are more equivalent to faith-based nonprofit leaders than the Samaritan.

The Levites and priests Jesus references were the religious professionals. Carrying out the unique tasks of the Church was in their job descriptions. Like most of us, they earned their living doing good work. It was their day job.

Still, they were too busy and too distracted to care about the person hurting on the street side. The Levite and the priest were not lazy. They weren't sitting in their homes, nor drowning their sorrows at a Hebrew watering hole. No, they were hustling, consumed by the work they had to do. So busy they ignored the work God had on the path in front of them. Focused on their religious duties, they were apathetic to the needs of others.

The example of the Samaritan motivates us to launch new ministries to serve the vulnerable. It compels many Christians to pursue work in homeless shelters, hospitals, jails, and orphanages. But in this parable, it is the Levite and priest who should serve as our gut check.

Early on in my (Chris's) career with HOPE, I remember attending a nonprofit conference in Washington, D.C. Populated by hundreds of peers from nonprofit organizations operating across the world, this should have been a venue where hope abounded.

The mood, though, was somber, as if the leaders in the room had resigned themselves to a life of cynicism. Speaker after speaker lamented the insurmountable challenges facing the world and facing their organizations. Apathy, sarcasm, and burnout marked even the casual conversations between sessions. When participants *did* exhibit sincerity from the stage or in conversation, it seemed like the members of the crowd patronized them for their naiveté. Cynicism reigned.

Now these were not lazy people. They were highly educated, talented, and accomplished nonprofit leaders. They had earned impressive degrees and racked up distinguished résumés. But the fire that brought them into this work had dimmed. While this was my first such experience, it was anything but the last.

The temptation to become a slothful leader lingers near us all. We can become preoccupied with everything *but* the bloody person lying in the ditch along our way. Adrift in policy discussions, office politics, and expense reports, we can easily develop a deep-set indifference to love's demands. Even more, as we're consumed by our own agendas, we can give up our attempts to work for change beyond our own organization's boundaries.

We've made the case throughout this book that we are a body, more powerful when we work in unison. We've argued the Kingdom will be strengthened as we find ways to root for our rivals, openhandedly offering the unique skills and resources with which God has blessed us.

As we come to believe these statements, we may be tempted to think the Kingdom needs us. But the truth is, we need the Kingdom. As Mordecai said to Esther, "If you keep silent at this time, relief and deliverance will rise for the Jews from another place, but you and your father's house will perish. And who knows whether you have not come to the kingdom for such a time as this?"[16] In Luke 19 Jesus strongly implies He can use rocks to accomplish His purposes, if not people.[17] How's that for a dose of humility?

As believers, we are privileged to know that God's Kingdom *is* coming. Our actions or inaction will not thwart it; we don't have that power. But when we fixate on our clan and fail to acknowledge the Kingdom as these cynical leaders did, we deprive ourselves of the joy and hope of understanding our part in what God is doing.

Many slothful leaders started out with a God-given call and grand ambitions. But as we focus on our clan and lose sight of the Kingdom beyond, we lose our perspective. Our drive to make a difference can become our undoing as the obstacles that are sure to come batter us and our resolve. We feel the enormous weight of our calling and forget that this burden is not ours to bear but rather rests on the shoulders of one who tells us to cast our cares upon Him.[18]

We will face funding shortfalls, corrupt governments, gut-wrenching injustices, and unforeseen setbacks. If we see only our clan, despairing apathy is a natural outgrowth of these circumstances. For those with a Kingdom perspective, however, even the worst days are tempered by the hope that there is a plan beyond our own. It isn't just us working for change but an all-powerful God working in and through us.

Slothful leaders fail to see that there's hope in not being the source of hope. There's hope in knowing that our shortcomings and mistakes aren't going to stop God's plan from going forward. Because of the Kingdom, there is hope.

Losing Our Will

A few years ago, I (Chris) sat with my wife, Alli, in a dimly lit conference room, awaiting an adoption and foster care presentation. We were giddy with excitement. This training was our first big step toward becoming foster parents. We had talked and prayed about it, but this was our moment to go public with our intent.

The trainer entered the room, connected her laptop to a projector, and launched into her presentation. Over the next three long hours, the trainer and a fellow employee at the adoption support agency lamented the challenges with the adoption and foster care systems, expounded on the worst-case scenarios for families, and crassly described the average costs incurred by adoptive and foster families. Our energy dropped with each passing minute.

Our foster care journey hit a major roadblock that night. We came into that training fervent to serve our city's most vulnerable children. We left uncertain about ourselves and about the system we hoped to work within. We experienced an organization embodying a laziness to love.

The adoption organization hosting the training began with noble ideals. It was focused on helping vulnerable children find safe homes. But this organization and its staff were not immersed in and enlivened by these ideals. The result was a sterile and patronizing session.

To us, it seemed this adoption organization had forgotten its reason for existence and had lost its will to love. Its leaders had succumbed to sloth, no longer caring enough to care after years of dealing with broken systems and people. The institution's website said the right things, but beyond the hopeful photos was an organization decaying from the inside out.

Institutions shape us: from the God-given institutions like the Church and the family to the institutions all around us—our schools, government agencies, recreation centers, businesses, and nonprofits. And if the world around us experiences faith-based organizations in the same way—as organizations that have given up on hope—we risk betraying the hope that is central to our faith.

A few months after our deflating training experience, we signed up for an introductory training with Project 1:27. We walked into a church auxiliary room nervous about what we might hear. We wanted foster care to be part of our story, but our confidence waned.[19]

The phrase "losing heart" originated as a reference to the anxious period between when a mother starts labor and before she delivers the baby.[20] Peter and I have both been beside our wives in those forever in-between moments. *Losing heart* gets it just right. I remember after a prolonged labor with our oldest son, I looked at our team of nurses, doctor, and midwife and mouthed, "Is this baby going to come out?"

I understood cognitively what would happen. One way or another, that baby would eventually make an appearance in the world. But after more than twenty-four hours in that hospital room, *I* was losing heart, though I tried my best not to let my wife know that! She was clearly the one doing the hard work.

But this is the anxious place where many faith-based leaders find ourselves. We know the significance of our work. We believe in the cause deep in our hearts. We know partnering with churches and other organizations enables significant and lasting change. And we want to care. But we're weary, forgetting why we got into this work in the first place. Sometimes it feels hard enough to care for our own clan, let alone concern ourselves with the Kingdom. Yet we've found the words of Proverbs 11:25 (NIV) to be true: "Whoever refreshes others will be refreshed." A Kingdom perspective may place demands on us, but it also renews our hope. When some of the earliest followers of Jesus were feeling discouraged, they received a letter of encouragement from the apostle Paul. Imagine how powerful and evocative these words must have been: "Let us not *lose heart* in doing good."[21]

Things are hard right now. But don't succumb to sloth. This work is worth it. Do not lose heart!

The Ongoing Task

At the Project 1:27 training, as soon as Shelly Radic opened her mouth, we knew this training would be different. Radic, the president of Project 1:27, shared vulnerably about her own calling to foster care. She described the joys and challenges of being an adoptive mom. She shared how God's heart for children explodes off the pages of our Scriptures. And she prayed with us. In fervor, she committed the decision we faced—to proceed as foster parents or not—to God in prayer.

She also made clear that no matter the outcomes, no matter the depth of heartache, no matter the isolation we'd feel, no matter the complications we might face with these vulnerable children and their biological parents—this work is worth it. She knew the pains and joys of being an adoptive mom firsthand.

This is the task of steadfast leaders and their organizations: to hold fast to our mission. As we do, it will compel us to link arms with other organizations running in the same direction. Slothfulness causes us to not put in the effort needed to collaborate. Steadfastness causes us to fight the gravitational forces drawing us into ourselves and pursue even inconvenient partnerships because of our unwavering commitment to our grander mission.

As a steadfast leader, Shelly Radic's fulfillment hinged on her obedience to do what God called her to do, not on the outcomes of her obedience. This is what she shared with us. Her steadfastness was not blind cheeriness. But it was resolute. This work mattered. And if not us, then who? Her call to action rooted itself in an enduring confidence in God's provision for *our* daily bread for the work ahead.

Just minutes into the training, Alli and I looked at one another, our eyes glistening, our hearts rekindled. This was what we wanted to be about. These were the reasons we wanted to open our family and our home to vulnerable children.

Project 1:27 is a faith-based organization making a big impact on families and children in Colorado and now across the country.[22] It's an organization that understands the magnitude of work to be done and accomplishes this work with passion and grace. Today, Project 1:27 is part of a network of churches, families, and nonprofits that have helped to dramatically decrease the number of children awaiting loving homes in Colorado.

"Recruiting families for . . . foster care and adoption is an ongoing task," Shelly Radic said in a radio interview. "Each time a new generation comes up, it's telling that story again and again. . . . The kids are there, and the heart of our responsibility as believers is to care for [them]."[23]

That night with Project 1:27 accelerated and enlivened our foster care journey. Radic understands the "ongoing task" and has not lost hope, despite new children being added to the foster care and adoption waiting lists each day. Enormous challenges face these children and the families who will care for them. But this is not a reason to despair. This is a reason to get to work.

Each of the foster children who have lived in our home did so because of the steadfastness of leaders like Shelly Radic. Her posture of hope gave us the confidence we needed to step forward.

Tightening Our Laces

Josh Heaston, Shelly Radic, and the Good Samaritan embody steadfastness. Their unwavering belief in God's redemptive work in the world animates their daily work. They are openhanded in their understanding of success, realizing they might never see their challenges "solved." There will be new YMCA leaders who do not know why George Williams founded the organization. There will be more children who enter the foster care system and more churches resistant to responding. And there will be more hurting people on the roadsides.

These steadfast leaders view the enormity of their task and the complexity of facing it as an opportunity, not a reason to give up hope.

In Psalm 61, David writes an honest prayer, expressing his weariness.

> "Hear my cry, O God,
>   listen to my prayer;
> from the end of the earth I call to you
>   when my heart is faint."[24]

In our work, there are daily moments when our hearts are faint. As leaders, we bear the weight of the challenges lingering inside and outside the walls of our organizations. But God invites us, like David, to bring these burdens to Him. Jesus invites us, "Come to me, all you who are weary and burdened, and I will give you rest."[25] And like David, when our bodies and hearts grow weary, we can take heart in the testimonies of the sisters and brothers who have gone before us.

"You have given me the heritage of those who fear your name," David writes.[26]

This is a gift to us too, a rich heritage of God's people who have faithfully, steadfastly followed Jesus into hard places. Remembering their witness through the ages and across the world can both enliven our spirits and add perspective to the challenges we face.

To fight the vice of sloth, steadfast leaders:

1. **Battle cynicism.** It's an easy outlet for nonprofit workers. But cynicism corrodes organizations, undermining the organization at every turn. It's easy to become cynical but hard to reverse cynicism once it begins to permeate the culture. At HOPE, one way we've tried to weed out cynicism is by cultivating a culture of direct conversation. Within faith-based organizations, it's easy for niceness to stifle honesty. When that happens, honest assessments instead simmer around water coolers and over email, often in the form of sarcasm. We do not do this perfectly, but we try to create an environment where our leaders both share and invite hard questions and honest criticisms.

2. **Remember their why.** Steadfast leaders renew their own enthusiasm for their work and create opportunities for their staff to do so as well. To foster a culture of steadfastness, leaders emphasize the heart of the mission. *New York Times* columnist David Brooks wrote that great organizations "tell and retell a sacred origin story about themselves."[27] They do so because their genesis story should inform the work they do today. These organizations seek every opportunity to ingrain this *why* into all aspects of their culture and rituals. In so doing, they insist remembering *why* is not a guarantee of achieving our desired results. Our *why* is about working toward the mission set before us, and that responsibility is true no matter the outcomes.

3. **Embrace the disciplines.** It's not coincidental that the first strategic priority for Heaston and the YMCA US Mission Network is to "reestablish prayer in the culture of the YMCA."[28] It's also no coincidence that Shelly Radic and Project 1:27 open their trainings in prayer. At HOPE, we pray and read Scripture corporately every Monday,

Wednesday, and Friday. Prayer *is* the work. Meditating on Scripture *is* the work. Singing together *is* the work. Taking communion *is* the work. Fasting corporately *is* the work. These disciplines shape us and shape our organizations. They're not extras but central to our identity and to our endurance. Steadfast leaders commit to prayer, fasting, worshiping, and saturating their work in God's Word. In *Acedia & Me*, Kathleen Norris writes, "Left unchecked, [sloth] can unravel the great commandment: as I cease to practice my love of God, I am also less likely to observe a proper love of my neighbor or myself."[29] Above all, faith-based nonprofit leaders need to help their organizations practice their shared love of God.

4. **Celebrate stability.** The earliest writing on sloth prescribed a confounding antidote for followers of Christ: *stability*.[30] It's an even more countercultural and timely prescription today. We live in an age of choice. Leaders can jump from organization to organization or job to job with ease. This luxury is a recent phenomenon. Human resources manager Ray Chung shared, "Industry trends show that if previously you had one job for a lifetime, today, you are likely to have ten."[31] Stability can be a by-product of slothfulness. But more often, stability is its antidote. Stability usually demands remaining steadfast and committed to laborious love. Steadfastness challenges employees not to see their jobs as stepping stones to something else. Steadfast leaders celebrate those who embody stability and create the sort of environment that makes staying attractive.

5. **Rally together.** Caring for the needs of over 140 million orphans worldwide doesn't just seem daunting; it seems impossible. Rather than growing discouraged, the Christian

Alliance for Orphans (CAFO) is a group of individuals, churches, and organizations committed to leaving their "logos and egos at the door" as they live out the call of Jesus to care for orphans and vulnerable children.[32] Today, under Jedd Medefind's leadership, the organization unites nearly 200 organizations and 650 churches by launching joint initiatives to bolster rates of adoption, foster care, and orphan care worldwide. Their website reads, "Without CAFO, many good ministries would still faithfully serve—yet often in isolation or even competition. Today, we get to see what is achieved when we labor together for a vision larger than any one of us could accomplish alone."[33] When we find ourselves losing heart, joining with others in pursuit of a common mission can refresh and renew our spirits. Working not for the glory of our organization but rather for the glory of God reminds us of our first love and reignites our passion.

REFLECTION QUESTIONS

1. Have you succumbed to a "laziness to love" and given up on passions and hopes, despairing about the enormity of a problem?
2. How can you renew enthusiasm for your work?
3. The Levite and priest were too busy to notice the need right in front of them. What is the need in front of you?

Conclusion

Is it possible for a faith-based nonprofit to actually put these ideas into practice? To believe in a world of abundance and practice radical generosity? To believe that our mission is not just to build an organization but to build the Kingdom of God? What might an organization that pursues Kingdom success over organizational success actually look like?

It might look like some of our closest rivals.

In 2005, as a still-green nonprofit leader, I (Peter) began meeting leaders of other faith-based microfinance institutions from all over the world. Over the next few years, I met remarkable leaders from the Dominican Republic, Rwanda, Moldova, the Philippines, Romania, and Burundi.

In each of these meetings, I met leaders from these countries who were further along in their understanding of microfinance. They all possessed a maturity of faith and a generosity of posture I hoped I could one day emulate.

And, to a person, they eschewed much of what I experienced elsewhere in the nonprofit sector. These leaders rooted for us. They were not haughty because of their success. They were not intimidated or envious of HOPE. They were not threatened by our interest in expanding into their sector. They were not protective of their expertise. They did not see us as rivals. They treated us like the family we are and engaged us as friends.

None of us are immune from pride, gluttony, greed, and the rest of the capital vices. But these leaders actively structured their systems, processes, and organizations to push back against these tendencies. They've organized their efforts *because* they're aware of their own personal and institutional tendencies to misdirected, excessive, and deficient love.

They've practiced the virtues we've written about in *Rooting for Rivals* and embody an abundance-minded, Kingdom-focused posture. This stance opened the door to partnership, as we came to believe we could do more together than we could do separately.

Today, we describe HOPE not as an organization but as a global *network*, comprising a number of autonomous organizations working hand in hand with each other. Our first official partner was Esperanza, a Dominican microfinance institution. Coincidentally and beautifully, *esperanza* is Spanish for *hope*, a regular reminder of the business we're in together.

"We could work alone," said Alexandra Nuñez, general director at Esperanza International, "but together, our work is better."[1]

Since 2005 we've been the beneficiaries of many partners who have joined with HOPE in unique and significant ways: Invest-Credit in Moldova, Center for Community Transformation in the Philippines, ROMCOM in Romania, and World Relief in Rwanda and Burundi. It's been more than microfinance institutions, though, who have thought and acted this way. Today we work with dozens of denominational and church partners all over the world, the first of which was the Anglican Church in Rwanda. The Chalmers Center and Opportunity International have been vital allies. Each of these organizations and their leaders has exhibited generosity and humility.

Through and with these friends, we've developed a renewed affection for the body of Christ and the joy of working side by side. Maintaining health in these partnerships has not always been easy, but it has been worth it. And it's been possible because of our shared recognition of our own sinfulness and our faith in the One who unites us.

Disciples as Rivals?

We don't know a lot about how Jesus chose His disciples. Some had been disciples of John the Baptist, others may have been relatives or acquaintances. But in the first Gospel, Matthew makes a point of telling us that Jesus brought together as associates and friends two men who would have been, under other circumstances, bitter rivals: Simon the Zealot and Matthew the tax collector.

Zealots were revolutionaries who took up arms against the Roman government. They were willing to kill or be killed to undermine the ruling authority. Tax collectors, on the other hand, were seen as betrayers of their own people, financing the government that controlled Israel and notoriously enriching themselves in the process.

We can only imagine the odd scene when Simon and Matthew were brought together and invited to follow Jesus. Over the next three years, and then to their death, these former rivals became co-laborers and friends working to advance God's Kingdom. They were united in the name of Jesus, and their love for Him bridged the divide between them.

As Scott Sauls writes, "Matthew's emphasis on a tax collector and a Zealot living in community suggests a hierarchy of loyalties, especially for Christians. Our loyalty to Jesus and His Kingdom must always exceed our loyalty to an earthly agenda, whether political or otherwise."[2]

Jesus did not come as a political messiah opposing Rome, yet His own disciples struggled to fathom (and regularly lost sight of) the reality that they were working for a heavenly Kingdom not an earthly cause. In Mark 9, the disciples argue about who is the greatest. In the next chapter of Mark, James and John come to Jesus with a bold request: when you have been glorified, allow us to sit at your right and left hand. They sought for themselves positions of honor and power within Christ's administration, and when the other disciples found out, they were justifiably indignant.

In both instances, Jesus gently reminds the disciples that His Kingdom is like nothing they have seen before. "Whoever would be great among you must be your servant," He tells them.[3] We follow our humble King and bring glory to His upside-down Kingdom when we serve one another, looking beyond ourselves to root for our rivals.

The two of us haven't always gotten this right. We regularly slip into old habits and close our hands tightly around what God has entrusted to us. But when we do get it right, we find it's not just good for the Kingdom, it's good for *us*. When we trust in our abundant God and think *Kingdom* and not *clan*, it's freeing. It renews our own souls and energizes our organization. In a strange way, the less consumed we've become with our own organization's notoriety and agenda, the healthier our organization has become.

When we fall into vices and small thinking, when we focus on our clan more than the Kingdom, and when our fearful eyes perceive scarcity instead of abundance, God's grace abounds. Just like the disciples, we find reminders of what our mission truly is. God used a Zealot and a tax collector, cowards and doubters, the selfish and the unseeing to take His message "to the ends of the earth."[4]

That same God invites us to lay aside our own agendas in pursuit of this higher calling. Fishermen and fanatics, preachers and practitioners, Jesus is still what unites us. We need each other in this journey. Let's be known as leaders who serve and glorify Christ through our radical generosity. Let's be people who long to see God's Kingdom come, even as our earthly kingdoms fade. And let's cheer one another on in the process.

We are in this together.

We are on the same team.

We are rooting for you.

Notes

Epigraph

1. Matthew 5:9 MESSAGE

Introduction

1. Cited by Thomas Pollak, program director at Urban Institute's National Center for Charitable Statistics, Michelle Ye Hee Lee, "Ben Carson's unsupported claim that 'nine out of 10 nonprofits fail,'" *The Washington Post*, October 26, 2015, https://www.washingtonpost.com/news/fact-check er/wp/2015/10/26/ben-carsons-unsupported-claim-that-nine-out-of-10-non profits-fail/?utm_term=.60c1bc57a935.

2. Clark Kerr, *The Uses of the University, 5th ed.*(Cambridge, MA: Harvard University Press, 2001), 115.

3. James 4:14

4. For the purposes of this book, we frequently refer to the body of Christ, including Christian nonprofits, as the Church. While we recognize that these entities are not one and the same, we see churches and Christian nonprofits as united in their call to fulfill the Great Commission and work toward "[God's] kingdom come...on earth as it is in heaven" (Matthew 6:10). Though their means are different, their end pursuit is similar; for that reason, we often address them jointly.

5. Luke 4:18

6. A.W. Tozer, *The Pursuit of God* (New York: Start Publishing LLC, 2012), e-book, 32.

7. Matthew 6:33, emphasis ours

8. Hebrews 12:1

9. Derek Kuykendall, interview with Chris Horst, July 24, 2017.

10. Kuykendall, interview.

11. Kuykendall, interview.

Chapter 1: Our Uncommon Unity

1. "Confidence in institutions," Gallup News, June 13, 2016, http://www.gallup.com/poll/1597/confidence-institutions.aspx.

2. "Rising Tide of Restrictions on Religion," Pew Research Center, September 20, 2012, http://www.pewforum.org/2012/09/20/rising-tide-of-restrictions-on-religion-findings/.

3. Beth Moore, *Breaking Free: Discover the Victory of Total Surrender* (Nashville: B&H Publishing Group, 2000), 123.

4. Mark Strauss, "It's Been 150 Years Since the U.S. Was This Politically Polarized," *Gizmodo*, June 12, 2014, https://io9.gizmodo.com/its-been-150-years-since-the-u-s-was-this-politically-1590076355.

5. "Directory of Charities and Nonprofit Organizations," Guidestar, http://www.guidestar.org/NonprofitDirectory.aspx?cat=8&subcat=44&p=1.

6. Jennifer Powell McNutt, "Division Is Not Always a Scandal," *Christianity Today*, December 30, 2016, http://www.christianitytoday.com/ct/2017/january-february/division-is-not-always-scandal.html.

7. 1 Corinthians 1:13

8. John 17:23

9. K.A. Ellis, "Standing as One," The Gospel Coalition, May 12, 2005, https://www.thegospelcoalition.org/article/standing-as-one.

10. John 13:35

11. Though we do see unity in Christ fading, we are also encouraged by Christians who, despite differing church traditions, seek to reverse this trend by joining together in unity. We recognize and celebrate these pioneers of unity and statements like the ECT (Evangelicals and Catholics Together: The Christian Mission in the Third Millennium).

12. Psalm 133:1

13. Les Yoder, lifelong Lancaster, PA, resident with Amish roots, discussion with Peter Greer, June 14, 2017.

14. Jon Guss, "Amish and Mennonite Groups in the Big Valley," *The Pennsylvania Center for the Book*, 2007, http://pabook2.libraries.psu.edu/palitmap/AmishInBigValley.html.

15. Charlie Kreider, discussion with Peter Greer, May 9, 2016.

16. Philip Gourevitch, *We Wish to Inform You That Tomorrow We Will Be Killed with Our Families: Stories from Rwanda* (New York: Farrar, Straus and Giroux, 1998), 55.

17. Paula Peñacoba, "Identified by Religion: Religion on National ID Cards," *Underground Network*, https://underground.net/identified-by-religion-religion-on-national-id-cards/.

18. Michele Wucker, *Why the Cocks Fight* (New York: Hill and Wang, 1999), 37, 49.

19. Christena Cleveland, *Disunity in Christ* (Downers Grove, IL: Inter-Varsity Press, 2013), 122–123.

20. Jeff Rutt, in discussion with Peter Greer, June 5, 2017.

21. Ephesians 6:12

22. Ajith Fernando, "The Way of Unifying Passion," July 24, 2017, https://www.youtube.com/watch?v=mgOn8rgBZlY.

23. Fernando, "The Way of Unifying Passion."

24. John Kania and Mark Kramer, "Collective Impact," *Stanford Social Innovation Review*, 2011, https://ssir.org/articles/entry/collective_impact.

25. Mike Brock, interview with Peter Greer, October 10, 2017.

26. "Pretzel Facts," How Stuff Works, accessed October 26, 2017, https://recipes.howstuffworks.com/pretzel-facts.htm.

27. Michael E. Porter, "Clusters and the New Economics of Competition," *Harvard Business Review*, November-December 1998, https://hbr.org/1998/11/clusters-and-the-new-economics-of-competition.

28. "About Us," Rising Tide Society, https://www.risingtidesociety.com/meet-us/.

29. Natalie Franke, "The Rising Tide Society," *Natalie Franke*, April 28, 2015, http://nataliefranke.com/2015/04/the-rising-tide-society/.

30. Further reading: Steven Weber, *The Success of Open Source* (Cambridge, MA: Harvard University Press, 2004).

31. Further reading: David Kinnaman and Gabe Lyons, *Good Faith: Being a Christian When Society Thinks You're Irrelevant and Extreme* (Grand Rapids, MI: Baker Books, 2016).

32. Scott Sauls, *Jesus Outside the Lines: A Way Forward for Those Who Are Tired of Taking Sides* (Carol Stream, IL: Tyndale House Publishers, 2015), 54.

33. Proverbs 27:17

Chapter 2: Kingdom over Clan

1. *The Founder*, directed by John Lee Hancock (2016; Los Angeles, CA: FilmNation Entertainment, 2017), DVD.

2. Eric Schlosser, *Fast Food Nation: The Dark Side of the All-American Meal* (New York: Houghton Mifflin, 2001), 37.

3. Haley Hamilton Cogill, "Postcard from Napa: Robert Mondavi Winery Turns 50," *D Magazine Partners*, May 31, 2016, https://www.dmagazine.com/food-drink/2016/05/postcard-from-napa-robert-mondavi-winery-turns-50/.

4. Dave McIntyre, "Fifty Years Ago, Robert Mondavi Transformed Napa Valley—And American Wine," *Washington Post*, July 23, 2016, https://www.washingtonpost.com/lifestyle/food/fifty-years-ago-robert-mondavi-transformed-napa-valley--and-american-wine/2016/07/23/615d4a06-4de3-11e6-aa14-e0c1087f7583_story.html?utm_term=.630c4ea03908.

5. Kip Davis, "Peter Mondavi Leads Krug's 150th Anniversary Celebration," *Napa Valley Register*, September 15, 2011, http://napavalleyregister

NOTES

.com/lifestyles/food-and-cooking/wine/peter-mondavi-leads-krug-s-th-anni
versary-celebration/article_94d0aed4-e013-11e0-8abb-001cc4c002e0.html.

6. Shawn Hubler, "Robert Mondavi, 94; Vintner was a Powerful Ambassador for California Wine," *Los Angeles Times*, May 17, 2008, http://www
.latimes.com/local/obituaries/la-me-mondavi17-2008may17-story.html.

7. James Laube, "Robert Mondavi Dies at Age of 94," *Wine Spectator*,
May 16, 2008, http://www.winespectator.com/wssaccess/show/id/40906.

8. Tracy Byrnes, "How Entrepreneur Robert Mondavi Changed Wine
Forever," *Entrepreneur Media*, accessed October 27, 2017, https://www.entre
preneur.com/article/253583.

9. Melanie Warner, "Constellation Agrees to Acquire Robert Mondavi
for $1 Billion," *New York Times*, last modified November 4, 2004, www
.nytimes.com/2004/11/04/business/constellation-agrees-to-acquire-robert
-mondavi-for-1-billion.html.

10. Catherine Clifford, "How a College Dropout Grew Whole Foods into
the Company Amazon is Buying for $13.7 Billion," *CNBC, LLC*, June 16,
2017, http://www.cnbc.com/2017/06/16/how-john-mackey-grew-whole-foods
-into-the-company-amazon-is-buying-for-13-point-7-billion.html.

11. "Whole Foods Market History," Whole Foods Market, accessed October 27, 2017, http://www.wholefoodsmarket.com/company-info/whole
-foods-market-history.

12. John Mackey, interview with Guy Raz, "Whole Foods Market: John
Mackey," *How I Built This*, May 14, 2017, https://one.npr.org/?sharedMedia
Id=527979061:528000104.

13. "Merger Consideration," Whole Foods Market, accessed October 27,
2017, http://investor.wholefoodsmarket.com/investors/press-releases/press-re
lease-details/2017/Amazon-to-Acquire-Whole-Foods-Market/default.aspx.

14. Paul R. La Monica and Chris Isidore, "Amazon Is Buying Whole Foods
for 13.7 Billion," *CNN Money*, June 16, 2017, http://money.cnn.com/2017
/06/16/investing/amazon-buying-whole-foods/index.html.

15. Like Mondavi, Mackey's leadership legacy looks a lot like most leaders': mixed. Among other criticisms, the most serious issue in his leadership
was his decision to anonymously criticize and undermine a rival company,
Wild Oats (a company Whole Foods would later acquire), http://www.nbc
news.com/id/19718742/ns/business-us_business/t/whole-foods-ceos-anony
mous-online-life/ and https://hbr.org/2007/07/who-is-the-real-john-mackey.

16. Dave Clouse, email communications with Peter Greer, August 26, 2017.

17. "Vacation Rental Site Lands $160M, Buys Competitor," *Austin Business Journal*, updated November 13, 2006, https://www.bizjournals.com
/austin/stories/2006/11/13/daily2.html.

18. Chance the Rapper, "Blessings," Apple Music, track 5 on *Coloring
Book*, 2016.

19. Terry Goodrich, "Faith-Based Organizations Shoulder Majority of
Crucial Services and Develop Creative Solutions for Homelessness, New

Baylor University Study Says," *Baylor*, February 1, 2017, http://www.baylor
.edu/mediacommunications/news.php?action=story&story=176953.

20. "The Halo Effect and the Economic Value of Faith-Based Organizations,"
Brookings, updated November 29, 2016, https://www.brookings.edu/events
/the-halo-effect-and-the-economic-value-of-faith-based-organizations/.

21. Brian Grim and Melissa Grim, "The Socio-Economic Contributions of
Religion to American Society: An Empirical Analysis," *Faith Counts*, http://
faithcounts.com/wp-content/uploads/Summary-Sheet.pdf.

22. "Research: A New Study Looks at the Significant Impact of Faith and
Religion in the United States," *Faith Counts*, accessed October 30, 2017,
http://faithcounts.com/Report/.

23. Paul Singer, "Faith Groups Provide the Bulk of Disaster Recovery, in
Coordination with FEMA," *USA Today*, September 10, 2017, https://www
.usatoday.com/story/news/politics/2017/09/10/hurricane-irma-faith-groups
-provide-bulk-disaster-recovery-coordination-fema/651007001/.

24. Andrea Palpant Dilley, "The Surprising Discovery about Those Co-
lonialist, Proselytizing Missionaries," *Christianity Today*, January 8, 2014,
http://www.christianitytoday.com/ct/2014/january-february/world-mission
aries-made.html.

25. "IMA World Health," Devex, updated 2017, https://www.devex.com
/organizations/ima-world-health-39693.

26. Faith Counts, "New Study Values Faith in America Over One Trillion
Dollars," *PR Newswire,* September 14, 2016, https://www.prnewswire.com
/news-releases/new-study-values-faith-in-america-over-one-trillion-dollars
-300328315.html.

27. Haley Smith, email communications with Peter Greer, September 28,
2017.

Chapter 3: Abundance over Scarcity

1. David Brooks, "How to Leave a Mark on People," *New York Times*,
April 18, 2017, https://www.nytimes.com/2017/04/18/opinion/how-to-leave
-a-mark-on-people.html.

2. Walter Brueggemann, "The Liturgy of Abundance, the Myth of Scarcity," *The Christian Century*, March 24, 1999, https://www.christiancentury
.org/article/2012-01/liturgy-abundance-myth-scarcity.

3. Melissa Russell, interview with Peter Greer, July 27, 2017.

4. John 6:9

5. Genesis 1

6. Genesis 11:29–30; 15:1–6; 18:9–15

7. Exodus 16

8. Mark 6:30–44

9. Ephesians 3:20 NIV

10. Julia Belluz, "The Truth about the Ice Bucket Challenge: Viral Memes
Shouldn't Dictate our Charitable Giving," *Vox*, August 20, 2014, https://

www.vox.com/2014/8/20/6040435/als-ice-bucket-challenge-and-why-we
-give-to-charity-donate.

   11. *Giving USA 2016: The Annual Report on Philanthropy for the Year 2015*, a publication of Giving USA Foundation, 2016, researched and written by the Indiana University Lilly Family School of Philanthropy.

   12. Luke 10:25

   13. Luke 10:29

   14. Initially available at http://muntherisaac.blogspot.com/2014/03/who -is-my-neighbor-my-talk-at-christ-at.html. Accessed January 2016 by Peter Greer.

   15. Chris Bruno and Matt Dirks, *Churches Partnering Together: Biblical Strategies for Fellowship, Evangelism, and Compassion* (Wheaton, IL: Crossway, 2014), 41.

   16. Mike Argento, "U.S. Attorney: York County 'the most violent' in central PA," *York Daily Record*, April 28, 2017, http://www.ydr.com/story/news/crime /2017/04/28/nine-indicted-gun-trafficking-violent-york-county/101003136/.

   17. Jim Tyson, interview with Peter Greer, June 2017.

Chapter 4: Seven Vices vs. Seven Virtues

   1. 2 Kings 4

   2. 1 Samuel 17

   3. Matthew 14:13–21

   4. HOPE International, "What's In Your Hands?", https://www.youtube .com/watch?v=vZlhYZgVMjk.

   5. Acts 13:22

   6. 1 Samuel 16:1–13

   7. 1 Samuel 16:13

   8. Matthew 25:40

   9. Rebecca Konyndyk DeYoung, *Glittering Vices* (Grand Rapids, MI: Brazos Press, 2009), 34.

   10. "The Traditional Enneagram," The Enneagram Institute, https://www .enneagraminstitute.com/the-traditional-enneagram/.

   11. "Which Deadly Sin Are You Guilty Of?" Buzzfeed, updated January 30, 2014, https://www.buzzfeed.com/juliapugachevsky/which-deadly-sin-are -you-guilty-of?utm_term=.up9dO14XK#.egvJnLzwD.

   12. St. Augustine, *Confessions*, as quoted in *Augustine's Conversion: A Guide to the Argument of Confessions I-IX* by Colin Starnes (Waterloo, Ontario: Wilfrid Laurier University Press, 1990), 230.

   13. St. Augustine, *On Christian Teaching*, trans. R.P.H. Green (Oxford: Oxford University Press, 2008), 21.

   14. DeYoung, *Glittering Vices*, 39.

   15. Genesis 41

   16. Interview with foundation executive, June 12, 2017. Interviewee requested that we keep his name confidential.

17. Sarah Eekhoff Zylstra, "Together for the Gospels: Unprecedented Unity Among Bible Translators Transforms Giving," *Christianity Today*, April 21, 2017, http://www.christianitytoday.com/ct/2017/may/together-for-gospels -bible-translation-unity-illuminations.html.

18. Zylstra, "Together for the Gospels."

19. "History is being made, right now. Be a part of it," YouVersion, updated May 8, 2017, http://blog.youversion.com/2017/05/history-made-right-now-part/.

Chapter 5: Pride vs. Humility

1. "Better Place press conference at 2009 Frankfurt Motor Show," Frankfurt Motor Show, September 15, 2009, https://www.youtube.com/watch?v =fIc9a5fG58Y.

2. Shai Agassi, "A new ecosystem for electric cars," TED2009, February 2009, https://www.ted.com/talks/shai_agassi_on_electric_cars#t-1063215.

3. Thomas L. Friedman, "While Detroit Slept," *New York Times*, December 9, 2008, http://www.nytimes.com/2008/12/10/opinion/10friedman.html.

4. Thomas L. Friedman, "Texas to Tel Aviv," *New York Times*, July 27, 2008, http://www.nytimes.com/2008/07/27/opinion/27friedman.html.

5. Shai Agassi (@sagassi), "You don't count on the wind to carry you . . . make your own wind and bring about change," Twitter, June 24, 2011, 2:45 p.m., https://twitter.com/sagassi/status/84376651370201090.

6. Max Chafkin, "A Broken Place: The Spectacular Failure of the Startup That Was Going to Change the World," *Fast Company*, April 7, 2014, https:// www.fastcompany.com/3028159/a-broken-place-better-place.

7. CBS, "Making the World a 'Better Place,'" March 19, 2009, YouTube video, 5:26, https://www.youtube.com/watch?v=mXfqGL3C2uI.

8. "Most Creative People 2009: Shai Agassi," *Fast Company*, updated May 8, 2009, https://www.fastcompany.com/3018888/4-shai-agassi.

9. CBS, "Making the World a 'Better Place.'"

10. CBS, "Making the World a 'Better Place.'"

11. Wired, "Agassi's Electric Car Grid," December 8, 2008, YouTube video, 27:59, https://www.youtube.com/watch?v=gNIijgJcsbs.

12. Shai Agassi, interview with Charlie Rose, December 1, 2010, https:// charlierose.com/videos/23770.

13. Clive Thompson, "Batteries Not Included," *New York Times*, April 16, 2009, http://www.nytimes.com/2009/04/19/magazine/19car-t.html.

14. Chafkin, "A Broken Place."

15. C.S. Lewis, *Mere Christianity* (New York: HarperCollins, 2001), 123.

16. Lewis, *Mere Christianity*, 122.

17. Dante Alighieri, *Purgatorio*, trans. Allen Mandelbaum (Berkeley: University of California Press, 1982), ix.

18. DeYoung, *Glittering Vices*, 29.

19. G.K. Chesterton, *The Common Man*, http://gkcdaily.blogspot.com /2013/07/if-i-had-only-one-sermon-to-preach.html.

20. Further reading: Peter Greer, *The Spiritual Danger of Doing Good* (Bloomington, MN: Bethany House, 2013), 19–27.

21. Lewis, *Mere Christianity*, 125.

22. Andrew Murray, *Humility* (Bloomington, MN: Bethany House, 2001), 16.

23. Genesis 4

24. Luke 9:46

25. Genesis 11:4

26. Esther 4:16

27. Esther 7:4

28. Esther 8:8

29. Chafkin, "A Broken Place."

30. "Sleeping With The Enemy," *Bloomberg Businessweek*, August 21, 2006, https://www.bloomberg.com/news/articles/2006-08-20/sleeping-with -the-enemy.

31. Chafkin, "A Broken Place."

32. Chafkin, "A Broken Place."

33. James 4:6

34. Adam Grant, "Are you a giver or a taker?," TED Institute, November 2016, https://www.ted.com/talks/adam_grant_are_you_a_giver_or_a_taker.

35. Acts 20:35

36. Chris Gough, personal interview with Chris Horst, May 4, 2017.

37. Greg Holder, *The Genius of One* (Colorado Springs, CO: Navpress, 2017), 64.

38. Gary Ringger, interview with Peter Greer, August 2, 2017.

39. "The Journey to Lifesong for Orphans," Lifesong for Orphans, accessed October 30, 2017, http://www.lifesongfororphans.org/about/the-journey/.

40. Gary Ringger, interview with Peter Greer, August 2, 2017.

41. J.K. Rowling, *Harry Potter and the Goblet of Fire* (New York: Scholastic Inc., 2000), 525.

42. Grant, "Are you a giver or a taker?"

43. The Build Network staff, "Why You Should Write an Annual Failure Report," *Inc.*, May 14, 2013, https://www.inc.com/thebuildnetwork/why-you -should-write-an-annual-failure-report.html.

44. "Pain in our work," Denver Institute for Faith and Work, 2017 annual report.

45. Together Chicago, "Who We Are," http://www.togetherchicago.com /who-we-are/#story.

46. Madeline Buckley, "Chicago homicides down 16 percent from 2016, but still surpass killings in recent past," *Chicago Tribune*, January 1, 2018, http://www.chicagotribune.com/news/local/breaking/ct-met-2017-crime -stats-20180101-story.html.

47. Fuller Theological Seminary website, "About Fuller," http://fuller.edu /about/mission-and-values/mission-beyond-the-mission/.

Chapter 6: Greed vs. Generosity

1. Rebecca Konyndyk DeYoung, *Glittering Vices* (Grand Rapids, MI: Brazos Press, 2009), 108.

2. Matt Egan, "5,300 Wells Fargo Employees Fired Over 2 Million Phony Accounts," *CNN Money*, September 9, 2016, http://money.cnn.com/2016/09/08/investing/wells-fargo-created-phony-accounts-bank-fees/index.html.

3. Mark Heath, interview with Peter Greer, August 2017.

4. DeYoung, *Glittering Vices*, 107.

5. Luke 11:3

6. Exodus 16

7. Proverbs 30:8–9

8. Exodus 16:20

9. Luke 12:21

10. Mike Pettengill, "God's Work, God's Way," *The Gospel Coalition*, May 21, 2015, https://www.thegospelcoalition.org/article/gods-work-gods-way.

11. 1 Corinthians 4:7

12. Patrick Hruby, "The Founding Fathers of Fantasy," *Sports on Earth*, December 2, 2013, http://www.sportsonearth.com/article/64244480/.

13. Cork Gaines, "The Number of People Playing Fantasy Sports is Skyrocketing," *Business Insider*, October 12, 2015, http://www.businessinsider.com/fantasy-sports-players-2015-10.

14. Lillian Kwon, "LifeChurch.tv Named Most Innovative Church," *The Christian Post*, January 18, 2007, http://www.christianpost.com/news/lifechurch-tv-named-most-innovative-church-25244/.

15. "One Church in Multiple Locations," Life.Church, accessed October 30, 2017, https://www.life.church/locations/?utm_source=life.church&utm_medium=website&utm_content=Header-Locations&utm_campaign=Life.Church.

16. "Reach More People for Christ," Life.Church, accessed October 30, 2017, https://www.life.church/churches/?utm_source=life.church&utm_medium=website&utm_content=MoreMenu-EquippingChurches&utm_campaign=Life.Church.

17. Jared Nelms, interview with Peter Greer, August 9, 2017.

18. Hebrews 10:24

19. Although we praise openhandedness throughout this book, we also recognize that open-sourcing materials has the unfortunate potential not only to weaken content but also to release authors and publishers from in-depth research and writing. Though celebrators of radical openhandedness, we are also strong believers in healthy competition, knowing that good competition often leads to higher-quality results. In short, we do not see openhandedness and competition as mutually exclusive, but rather see both as integral to organizations living out an abundant, Kingdom-focused mentality.

20. "Resource Library," HOPE International, accessed October 30, 2017, http://www.hopeinternational.org/resources.

21. Jane Jacobs, *The Death and Life of Great American Cities* (New York: Vintage Books, 1992), 34.

22. Joshua 3–4

23. 1 Samuel 7:12

24. Interview, October 12, 2017. Interviewee requested to remain anonymous.

25. Todd Kemp, donor and trip participant with Face of Justice Ministries, interview with Chris Horst, October 30, 2017.

26. Tim Keller, "Why Plant Churches?," https://www.redeemercitytocity.com/s/Why-Plant-Churches.pdf.

27. "Regions," Redeemer City to City, accessed October 30, 2017, https://www.redeemercitytocity.com/regions/.

28. North Point Media, "Be Rich Celebration 2016," Vimeo, 5:37, https://vimeo.com/193775835.

Chapter 7: Gluttony vs. Temperance

1. Mark Miller (CFA vice president of high performance leadership), interview with Peter Greer, October 20, 2017.

2. Tim Keller, "Gluttony; The Case of Achan," sermon, March 5, 1995, https://gospelinlife.com/downloads/gluttony-the-case-of-achan-6374/.

3. Larry Gordon, "Stanford University President John L. Hennessy to Leave Office Next Year," *Los Angeles Times*, June 11, 2015, http://www.latimes.com/local/education/la-me-ln-stanford-president-20150611-story.html.

4. Malcolm Gladwell, interview with John Hennessy, *Revisionist History*, "My Little Hundred Million," podcast audio, July 21, 2016, http://revisionisthistory.com/episodes/06-my-little-hundred-million.

5. Jim Collins, *How the Mighty Fall* (New York: HarperCollins, 2009), 45.

6. Venessa Wong, "Chick-fil-A Stole KFC's Chicken Crown With a Fraction of the Stores," *Bloomberg*, March 28, 2014, https://www.bloomberg.com/news/articles/2014-03-28/chick-fil-a-stole-kfcs-chicken-crown-with-a-fraction-of-the-stores.

7. Latif Lewis Williams, "CEO's Corner: Chick-fil-A's Dan Cathy on Rising Food Costs, Family Values," AOL, July 8, 2011, https://www.aol.com/article/2011/07/08/ceos-corner-chick-fil-a-dan-cathy-food-costs-family-values/19985964/.

8. Brian Solomon, "Meet David Green: Hobby Lobby's Biblical Billionaire," *Forbes*, September 18, 2012, https://www.forbes.com/sites/briansolomon/2012/09/18/david-green-the-biblical-billionaire-backing-the-evangelical-movement/+&cd=2&hl=en&ct=clnk&gl=us.

9. Witold Rybczynski, *A Clearing in the Distance: Frederick Law Olmsted and America in the Nineteenth Century* (New York: Scribner, 1999), 385.

10. Linnea Spransy, "Systems and Chaos," Q Ideas, http://qideas.org/videos/systems-and-chaos/.

11. Legacy Disciple, "Sho Baraka & Propaganda on Faith and Politics," September 26, 2016, YouTube video, 29:05, https://www.youtube.com/watch?v=ATxnG9SBVC8.

12. Benj Petroelje, "Lines and Lines Athwart Lines: Givenness, Limits, and the Practice of Sport," *The Other Journal*, August 22, 2016, https://the otherjournal.com/2016/08/22/lines-lines-athwart-lines-givenness-limits -practice-sport/.

13. Matthew 9:15

14. Philippians 3:19

15. Jen Pollock Michel, *Keeping Place* (Downers Grove, IL: InterVarsity Press, 2017), 163.

16. Walter Elwell, "Feasts and Festivals of Israel," *Baker's Evangelical Dictionary of Theology*, 1997, https://www.biblestudytools.com/dictionar ies/bakers-evangelical-dictionary/feasts-and-festivals-of-israel.html.

17. John 2:1–11

18. Revelation 19:6–9

19. Leviticus 23

20. Genesis 18

21. Luke 15:20–24

22. Luke 15:32

23. Rebecca Konyndyk DeYoung, *Glittering Vices* (Grand Rapids, MI: Brazos Press, 2009), 15.

24. "Our Vision," Praxis, accessed October 30, 2017, http://www.praxi slabs.org/vision/.

25. Greg Brenneman, email communication with Peter Greer, January 27, 2018.

Chapter 8: Lust vs. Love

1. J.R.R. Tolkien, *The Two Towers* (New York: Houghton Mifflin Harcourt, 2004), 613.

2. *The Lord of the Rings: The Two Towers*, directed by Peter Jackson (2002; Burbank, CA: New Line Cinema, 2003), DVD.

3. *The Lord of the Rings: The Return of the King*, directed by Peter Jackson (2003; Burbank, CA: New Line Cinema, 2004), DVD.

4. Tim Keller, https://mobile.twitter.com/timkellernyc/status/93371275 6259328000.

5. Thomas Aquinas, *De Caritate a.3; Summa Theologiae II-II*, q.23, a.8.

6. Colossians 3:14; 1 Corinthians 13:13

7. In *You Are What You Love: The Spiritual Power of Habit* (Grand Rapids, MI: Brazos Press, 2016), James K.A. Smith offers helpful analysis on this topic.

8. 1 Kings 16:30, 33

9. 1 Kings 21:2

10. 1 Kings 20:43

11. 1 Kings 21:7

19. Fred Smith, "Push Me and I'll Push Back," *The Gathering*, September 28, 2017, https://thegathering.com/push-me-and-ill-push-back/.

20. Martin Luther King Jr., *The Radical King*, ed. Cornel West (Boston: Beacon Press, 2015), 56, 60.

21. Linda Wertheimer, "'Team of Rivals': Lincoln's Political Prowess" National Public Radio, November 5, 2005, http://www.npr.org/templates /story/story.php?storyId=93790272.

22. Doris Kearns Goodwin, *Team of Rivals: The Political Genius of Abraham Lincoln* (New York: Simon & Schuster, 2005), 8.

23. Robert Greene and Joost Elffers, *The 48 Laws of Power* (New York: Penguin Group, 1998), 12.

24. Doris Kearns Goodwin, interview with Terry Gross, *Fresh Air*, "Lincoln by Goodwin: 'Political Genius,'" podcast audio, November 8, 2005, https:// www.npr.org/templates/story/story.php?storyId=4994044.

25. Doris Kearns Goodwin, *Team of Rivals: The Political Genius of Abraham Lincoln* (New York: Simon & Schuster, 2005), 6.

26. Maria Konnikova, "The Lost Art of the Unsent Angry Letter," *New York Times*, March 22, 2014, https://www.nytimes.com/2014/03/23/opinion /sunday/the-lost-art-of-the-unsent-angry-letter.html.

27. James M. McPherson, "'Team of Rivals': Friends of Abe," *New York Times*, November 6, 2005, http://www.nytimes.com/2005/11/06/books/review /team-of-rivals-friends-of-abe.html.

28. Peter Greer and Chris Horst, *Mission Drift: The Unspoken Crisis Facing Leaders, Charities, and Churches* (Bloomington, MN: Bethany House Publishers, 2014).

29. John 13

30. Luke 10:25–37

31. Book of Hosea

32. Matthew 10:16

33. John Inazu, "Pluralism Doesn't Mean Relativism," *Christianity Today*, April 6, 2015, http://www.christianitytoday.com/ct/2015/april-web-only/plur alism-doesnt-mean-relativism.html?start=4. For more, see John's great book *Confident Pluralism*, and *Free to Serve* by Stanley Carlson-Thies and Stephen Monsma.

34. Genesis 22:18

35. Andy Crouch, "Speak Truth to Trump," *Christianity Today*, October 10, 2016, http://www.christianitytoday.com/ct/2016/october-web-only/speak -truth-to-trump.html.

36. 1 Corinthians 15:33

37. C.S. Lewis, *Prince Caspian Movie Tie-in Edition* (New York: Harper-Collins, 2002), 179, 80.

38. Lewis, *Prince Caspian*, 80.

39. Lewis, *Prince Caspian*, 80.

40. Evan Low and Barry Corey, "We First Battled Over LGBT and Religious Rights. Here's How We Became Unlikely Friends," *Washington Post*, March 3, 2017, https://www.washingtonpost.com/news/acts-of-faith/wp/2017/03/03/we-first-battled-over-lgbt-and-religious-rights-heres-how-we-became-unlikely-friends/?utm_term=.418d300209d0.

41. Kathryn Joyce, *The Child Catchers: Rescue, Trafficking, and the New Gospel of Adoption* (New York: PublicAffairs, 2013).

42. Kathryn Joyce, "The Evangelical Orphan Boom," *New York Times*, September 21, 2013, http://www.nytimes.com/2013/09/22/opinion/sunday/the-evangelical-orphan-boom.html.

43. Ashley Phelan, "Conflict, Critique, and Civility: A Public Conversation with Kathryn Joyce and Jedd Medefind," CAFO, January 30, 2017, https://cafo.org/workshop/conflict-critique-civility-public-conversation-kathryn-joyce-jedd-medefind/.

Chapter 11: Sloth vs. Steadfastness

1. Josh Heaston, personal communication with Chris Horst, March 2014.

2. J.E. Hodder Williams, *The Life of Sir George Williams: Founder of the Young Men's Christian Association* (Cambridge, MA: The University Press, 1906), 96.

3. Frederick Buechner, *Wishful Thinking: A Seeker's ABC* (New York: Harper & Row, 1973), 89.

4. Rebecca Konyndyk DeYoung, "The Seven Deadly Sins: Sloth," Wheaton College Address, November 4, 2015, https://www.youtube.com/watch?v=-2RURCKxGGI.

5. William Willimon, "Sloth as Slow Suicide," *The Other Journal*, October 18, 2007, https://theotherjournal.com/2007/10/18/sloth-as-slow-suicide/.

6. Proverbs 13:4

7. *Glittering Vices* and Christ Central Church series (Durham), http://www.christcentraldurham.com/7-deadly-sins/, among others.

8. "Who We Are," US Mission Network, accessed October 30, 2017, https://usmissionnetwork.org/who-we-are/.

9. "Our Leadership," US Mission Network, accessed October 30, 2017, https://usmissionnetwork.org/our-leadership/.

10. Josh Heaston, interview with Chris Horst, April 2014.

11. Robert Gelinas, "Seven Deadly Sacraments: Part 4," March 12, 2017, https://www.youtube.com/watch?v=K1cPMiFjlJo&t=349s.

12. Josh Heaston, email communications with Chris Horst.

13. DeYoung, *Glittering Vices*, 94.

14. Dorothy L. Sayers, *The Other Six Deadly Sins: An Address Given to the Public Morality Council at Caxton Hall, Westminster on October 23, 1941*, http://www.lectionarycentral.com/trinity07/sayers.html.

15. Luke 10:33–34

16. Esther 4:14

17. Luke 19:40

18. 1 Peter 5:7

19. Chris Horst, "Institutions Matter More Than You Think," *The Ethics and Religious Liberty Commission*, http://erlc.com/resource-library/articles/institutions-matter-more-than-you-think.

20. "Final Instructions," Blue Letter Bible, accessed October 30, 2017, https://www.blueletterbible.org/Comm/guzik_david/StudyGuide_Gal/Gal_6.cfm.

21. Galatians 6:9 NASB, emphasis ours.

22. "Current 1.27 Ministries," Project 1.27, accessed October 30, 2017, http://project127.com/1-27-network/current-1-27-ministries/.

23. Shelly Radic, "Shelly Radic Interviewed on Adoption Perspectives," http://project127.com/news/shelly-radic-interviewed-adoption-perspectives/, recording broadcast from 670AM KLTT on September 6, 2014.

24. Psalm 61:1–2

25. Matthew 11:28 NIV

26. Psalm 61:5

27. David Brooks, "How to Leave a Mark on People," *New York Times*, April 18, 2017, https://www.nytimes.com/2017/04/18/opinion/how-to-leave-a-mark-on-people.html.

28. Josh Heaston, phone interview with Chris Horst, April 2017.

29. Kathleen Norris, *Acedia & Me: A Marriage, Monks, and a Writer's Life* (New York: Riverhead Books, 2010), 113.

30. DeYoung, "The Seven Deadly Sins: Sloth."

31. Ray Chung, email communications with Peter Greer, September 2017.

32. Christian Alliance for Orphans, "About Us," https://cafo.org/about/.

33. Christian Alliance for Orphans, "About Us."

Conclusion

1. https://www.instagram.com/p/BYQtxYtgMpc/?taken-by=hope_intl.

2. Scott Sauls, *Befriend: Create Belonging in an Age of Judgment, Isolation, and Fear* (Carol Stream, IL: Tyndale House Publishers, 2015), 212.

3. Matthew 20:26

4. Acts 13:47

Acknowledgments

Once again, we were surrounded by colleagues, friends, and family who rooted for us as we wrote this book. To each who invested time and talent in shaping this message, thank you! Andy McGuire, Sharon Hodge, and the Bethany House team. Just like with *Mission Drift*, you believed in this message and guided us each step of the journey.

Andrew Wolgemuth and the team at Wolgemuth & Associates. You are far more than just competent literary agents, you are our friends, advisers, and brothers in Christ.

To our editorial and support team, who offered constructive criticism and countless edits and improvements. Brianna Lapp went above and beyond, investing so much into this book. Special thanks also to Madi Burke, Tim Høiland, Benj Petroelje, Lindsay Robinson, Ray Chung, Amie Davis, Janice Seibert, Haley Smith, Becca Spradlin, Claire Stewart, Tom Lin, and David Bronkema.

Leaders of rival organizations who have modeled uncommon generosity, including Dave Valle, Carlos Pimentel Sanchez, Alex Nuñez, Ruth Callanta, Ghena Russu, Vlad Mihut, Brian Fikkert, Scott Arbeiter, Jeff Galley, Russ Mask, Michael Briggs,

Atul Tandon, David Morgan and Roxanne de Graaf at Partners Worldwide, and Archbishop Onesphore Rwaje of the Anglican Church of Rwanda.

The Board of Directors at HOPE International, who encouraged us to write this book and model radical generosity.

Wess Stafford, Mart Green, Todd Peterson, Greg Holder, Phill Butler, Tom Lin, and Eddie Waxer, leaders who have consistently rooted for their rivals and been generous with their time throughout this project.

Our families: Laurel, Keith, Lili, and Myles. And Alli, Desmond, Abe, and Juni. We love you and are your biggest fans.

Peter Greer is president and CEO of HOPE International, a global Christ-centered microenterprise development organization serving throughout Africa, Asia, Latin America, and Eastern Europe.

Prior to joining HOPE, Peter worked internationally as a microfinance advisor in Cambodia and Zimbabwe, and served as managing director of Urwego Bank in Rwanda. He is a graduate of Messiah College and Harvard University's Kennedy School.

Peter is an author and speaker, and has a passion to see the Church engage in effective missions and economic development. He has written *The Poor Will Be Glad* (with Phil Smith, 2009), *The Spiritual Danger of Doing Good* (with Anna Haggard, 2013), *Mission Drift* (with Chris Horst, 2014 and selected as a 2015 Book Award Winner by *Christianity Today*), *Entrepreneurship for Human Flourishing* (with Chris Horst, 2014), *Watching Seeds Grow* (with his son Keith, 2014), *The Giver and the Gift* (with David Weekley, 2015), *40/40 Vision* (with Greg Lafferty, 2015) *Created to Flourish* (with Phil Smith, 2016), and *The Board and the CEO* (with David Weekley, 2017). Currently, Peter serves as the entrepreneur-in-residence at Messiah College and as a Praxis Venture Partner.

More important than his occupation is his role as husband to Laurel and dad to Keith, Lilianna, and Myles.

Visit www.peterkgreer.com for more information or connect with him on social media at @peterkgreer.

Chris Horst is the vice president of development at HOPE International, where he employs his passion for advancing initiatives at the intersection of faith and work. In addition to his role at HOPE, Chris spends an alarming percentage of his free time tending to his yard with all the loving care normally afforded to newborn children. He and his wife, Alli, have three human children of whom they are even prouder than they are of their lawn—Desmond, Abe, and June. As a dad to three kiddos, Chris has recently undergone a radical transformation from self-proclaimed foodie to a man who prepares far more trays of chicken nuggets than avocado toast. He wouldn't change it.

Chris serves on the boards of the Denver Institute for Faith & Work and the Mile High WorkShop and is a founder of dadcraft.com. He loves to write, having been published in *The Denver Post* and *Christianity Today* and co-authored *Mission Drift, Entrepreneurship for Human Flourishing*, and *Rooting for Rivals* with Peter Greer. *Mission Drift* was named a book of the year in 2015 by *Christianity Today*; *WORLD Magazine* and the Evangelical Christian Publishers Association honored it as a book of the year runner-up and finalist, respectively. Chris was a very average student, but he did graduate with both a bachelor's degree from Taylor University and an MBA from Bakke Graduate University.

Jill Heisey is a freelance communications specialist. She graduated from Messiah College with degrees in politics and Spanish before landing her dream job as a member of HOPE International's marketing team.

She and her husband, Bryan, are parents to Adelyn and Celia and live in Frederick, Maryland, where Jill spends her days writing anything from books and marketing materials to the ABCs.

About HOPE International

HOPE International invests in the dreams of families in the world's underserved communities as we proclaim and live the gospel. We provide discipleship, biblically based training, savings services, and small loans, empowering women and men to use the skills God has placed in their hands to provide for their families and strengthen their communities.

For specific resources on HOPE International's approach to spiritual integration, operations, fundraising, governance, or if there are ways we can root for you, visit our online resource portal at www.hopeinternational.org/resources.

Proceeds of this book support HOPE International and other "rival" organizations.

More from the Authors

Visit peterkgreer.com for a full list of their books.

Why do so many organizations wander from their mission, while others remain Mission True? Can drift be prevented? In *Mission Drift*, HOPE International executives Peter Greer and Chris Horst show how to determine whether your organization is in danger of drift. You'll discover what you can do to prevent drift or get back on track and how to protect what matters most.

Mission Drift

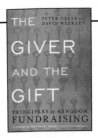

What happens when Christian ministry and social justice lead to burnout, pride, or worse? Peter Greer knows firsthand how this can happen. Using stories from his own life and the lives of others in ministry, Greer shows everyone from CEOs to weekend volunteers how to protect themselves from the unseen hazards of doing good works and how to keep the flame of passionate ministry burning brightly.

The Spiritual Danger of Doing Good

Peter Greer and philanthropist David Weekley share a countercultural, relational approach to fundraising. Unlike guilt-inducing gimmickry, their model inspires generosity with a Kingdom perspective that values the giver and the receiver.

The Giver and the Gift

BETHANYHOUSE